Herb Garden on the Green of Central
Moravian Church, Bethlehem, Pennsylvania

THE HERB GARDEN

by
Dorothy Bovee Jones

DORRANCE & COMPANY
Philadelphia

FOR EDNA:
ONLY SISTER, BEST FRIEND, AND
CONSTANT INSPIRATION, THROUGH
ALL THE YEARS

CONTENTS

Page

CHAPTER

A GARDEN OF HERBS NEED BE NO LARGER THAN THE SHADOW OF A BUSH, YET WITHIN IT, AS IN NO OTHER, A MOOD OF THE EARTH APPROACHES AND ENCOUNTERS THE SPIRIT OF MAN.

BENEATH THESE ANCESTRAL LEAVES, THESE IMMEMORIAL ATTENDANTS OF MAN, THESE SERVANTS OF HIS MAGIC AND HEALERS OF HIS PAIN, THE EARTH UNDERFOOT IS THE EARTH OF POETRY AND THE HUMAN SPIRIT. IN THIS SMALL SUN AND SHADE FLOURISHES A WHOLE TRADITION OF MANKIND.

Henry Beston
Herbs and the Earth

ACKNOWLEDGEMENTS

I should like to say thank you to:

my son-in-law, Paul W. Dale, who persuaded me to get to work on the second edition of *The Herb Garden*;

my daughter, Dorothy Dale, for her masterly proofreading of the manuscript;

my sister, Edna J. Dorsey, for designing the jacket of the book, and several of the line drawings;

Professor William J. Eney, and John Gera, of the John Fritz Engineering Laboratory of Lehigh University, for making the final drawing of the Expanding Herb Garden, and for updating the drawing of the Herb Garden on the Green;

the New York Public Library, for assistance beyond the call of duty;

the Morgan Library, which has been a treasure trove for me for years;

the Hunt Botanical Library, which I visited first in 1956, when the library was still housed at the home of Mr. and Mrs. Hunt in Pittsburgh. I have visited it many times since then in its new home at Carnegie-Mellon University in Pittsburgh.

Gourmet Magazine, for permission to use its authentic recipe for kulich, which I have changed only enough to make it a little easier to achieve with readily available equipment.

* * * * *

In writing or talking about herbs, I never get far without quoting Henry Beston. My copy of the first edition of *Herbs and the Earth* is a precious possession. In it, he has expressed more of what the herbs mean to me than any other writer, ancient or modern.

I am happy to remember the day when we made our way into the back country in Maine, so that I could shake hands with Henry Beston. I am grateful to his publishers, Doubleday and Co, Inc., for permission to quote a few passages from *Herbs and the Earth*.

Dorothy Bovee Jones

INTRODUCTION TO THE SECOND EDITION OF
THE HERB GARDEN

In 1947 I wrote a little book called *The Herb Garden*, at the request of a publisher who had visited and enjoyed the small herb garden on the Green of the Central Moravian Church in Bethlehem, Pennsylvania.

This was a sketch, based on my experience and reading of a good many years, set down to show some of the rewards that come from the cultivation of an herb garden. It suggested a simple approach for those readers who might be persuaded to find, in the growing and using of herbs, not only a source of great interest and pleasure, but also the continuance of an ancient tradition.

The day that little book went out of print remains an exciting day in my life. All day I received telephone calls from people who had tried to buy a copy, and had been told there was none to be had. They all seemed to feel that by telling me about it, something could be done.

That day is now a long time ago, and I have always meant to do something about it. Publishing a duplicate edition would always have been easy, but even by the time the book went out of print, there were changes I wanted to make. There were, first of all, a few errors that needed correction.

Beyond that, I had learned more about herbs, and more about life. Years inevitably bring grief as well as happiness, and I had found that there is therapy in the soil, and especially in the soil in which herbs grow.

* * * * *

The little garden on the Green is reminiscent of the interest in herbs that existed in early Bethlehem. Bishop Levering, in his *History of Bethlehem*, reports that in March 1747 an extensive garden was laid out, with the understanding that a portion of it should be devoted to growing medicinal herbs for the laboratory and pharmacy. The Simon Rau Drug Store had opened in 1743, and dispensed many medicines made from the herbs grown in that garden. In 1947, when I wrote *The Herb Garden*, that drug store was still serving patrons, but today the "Old Apothecary Shop" is a museum, administered by the Moravian Church.

Although for years the interest in herbs has been increasing, it has now reached new heights. People of all ages and of all walks of life find a common meeting ground in the study of these historic plants. Garden clubs search for speakers who will talk to them about herbs, and a visit to an herb garden is a high point in the year's program.

Grade school pupils choose projects involving the study of herbs, sometimes covering a long period.

High school and college students find, in the use of herbs, and especially in the drinking of herb teas, a charming expression of the simple life they so highly regard, and of their admirable concern for eating natural, healthful food. Indeed, as I put this book together, I had in mind many charming young friends, who are just beginning to feel a deep interest in the herbs. I hope very much that this book will please and help them.

Like the first edition, this book is primarily for people with a newly-acquired interest in herbs, who want to know what to plant. Chapter II, "The Beginner's Herb Garden," especially is for them. This list of twelve basic culinary herbs is a good starting point. Most people want to plant first some herbs which they can use in the kitchen.

However, the readers on whom these fascinating plants have really cast their spell will soon go farther. They will discover, from adventures with precious old books in great libraries, from talks with other herb growers, from visits to gardens near and far, but most of all from intimate acquaintance with the herbs themselves, that this is a field of enchantment. It is limited in scope only by the facts that one's planting space usually has boundaries, and that there are, alas, only twenty-four hours in each day.

I

THE HERB GARDEN

Awake, O north wind; and come, thou South; blow upon my garden, that the spices thereof may flow out.

Song of Solomon 4:16

Summer in Pennsylvania is a lavish and productive season, from the first winter aconite to the last saffron crocus. Because it is so beautiful, it always seems too short, and we look for ways of extending the enjoyment of our gardens.

Even a small planting of fragrant herbs can make a real contribution to this endeavor, because an herb garden dispenses year-round benefits. It wakens early in the spring to provide new zest for the salad bowl from the fresh leaves of tarragon and the first green shoots of chives. From early spring until long after the first frost, one never comes back from the herb garden empty-handed. There are always flowers and fragrant foliage for the house and for friends; fresh seasonings for the meat loaf, sorrel for soup, and Alpine strawberries. Late in the autumn, the herb gardener surveys with satisfaction the pantry shelves. Rows of small glass jars hold dried herbs for seasoning, leaves and aromatic seeds; there are herbs for beverages, and jars of sparkling herb-flavored jellies. Glass-stoppered bottles hold clear herb-flavored vinegars, in lovely colors, each bottle with its identifying leaf.

Clippings from the herbs have been saved all summer—clippings too woody for the compost pile, too fragrant to throw away. Tied in firm bunches, they make useful little faggots for starting autumn fires in the grate. They still hold the fragrance of rosemary, bay, lavender, and sage.

On the table in the guest room stands a pottery bowl. All

1

through the summer it has been receiving tip cuttings with the flowers of each herb as it came into bloom at the peak of its fragrance—sweet woodruff, lavender, rosemary, the green and purple basils, the santolinas, and many others. Now and then a few sweet violets, a Johnny-jump-up, a pot marigold, or a rosebud added its color to the mixture, which will retain its summer fragrance all through the winter, to delight everyone who smells it.

In the linen closet, sheets and pillow cases are absorbing the sweet odor of lavender flowers, in cheesecloth bags. On a south windowsill stand some herb plants which will spend the winter indoors with the scented geraniums, the dittany of Crete, the pineapple sage, the *salvia dorisiana*, and the trailing rosemary. Fortunate is the owner of handsome, hand-made terra-cotta pots to hold them. The soft red of these pots is a perfect complement to the gray of Cretan dittany, the dark green of rosemary.

WHAT ARE THESE HERBS?

Botanically, an herb is a soft-stemmed plant which dies down to the ground every fall. However, in 1629 John Parkinson, an apothecary of London, wrote a definition which has become a classic. "Herbs," he said, "are fit for Meat or Medicine; for Use, or for Delight." So, using his definition, without any regard for the botanical significance of the name, any plant is an herb if it has a history of use, as a seasoning, a perfume, a medicine, or as an aid to good housekeeping. It may be a bulb, or a shrub, or a vine; it may have soft stems or woody; it may be annual or perennial; it may hold its leaves in winter, or drop them. Even a tree may be an herb, as is the linden, from whose flowers and leaves the French make a tisane called *tilleul*. Just as noble an herb is the tiny, trailing Corsican mint, whose flowers are so small that they are invisible to a person looking down at them from a standing position.

The herbs are the workers of the plant kingdom. They have a long human history because, through the ages, men have carried the herbs with them, wherever they traveled, across the world. What man would leave behind a plant that would insure him a safe journey, protect him from pestilence and witchcraft and the Evil Eye, heal his illnesses, and make his heart merry? Herbs were used in religious ceremonies, to flavor and preserve food, to heal every wound and to bury the dead.

Their history goes back hundreds and sometimes thousands of years, to Egypt, to India, to ancient China. Schools of herbalists existed as early as 3000 B.C. in Egypt. In 400 B.C. Hippocrates taught the use of herbs for human ailments, and many of the plants he used are still in use today.

In the second half of the first century of our era, Pedanius Dioscorides, who is probably the greatest of the ancient herbalists, compiled a list of about 400 herbs which is known as *De Materia Medica*. He gave the name of the plant, its habitat, the directions for its use as medicine, and its medicinal effects. He was a physician attached to the Roman army, and was able to collect information about plants right in the field. The original five-volume manuscript was worn out or lost or destroyed, but the work was so valuable that it was copied constantly through the years, and as time went on illustrations began to appear in it. The herbal of Dioscorides depends largely upon the work of the men who had preceded him in his own field—Hippocrates, Theophrastus, and many other botanists and herbalists. For more than thirteen centuries, his *De Materia Medica* was the principal text-book of herbalists and physicians throughout the civilized world. Many of the medicines he mentioned are still included in the pharmacopoeias of Europe and America, among them aloes, anise seed, belladonna, chamomile, cardamom, coriander, linseed, licorice and peppermint.

During the occupation of Britain, the Romans cultivated many herbs which Caesar's armies had carried with them from their native Mediterranean shores. They knew and used chives, parsley, rue, rosemary, southernwood, borage, and thyme. They boasted that they needed no doctors, because there was an herb for every human ill.

At a later date, these herbs were called "simples," and still later, the Doctrine of Signatures came into favor. Each plant was thought to show, by its color or form, or habit of growth, the use for which it was intended. *Pulmonaria*, or lungwort, showed by its leaves, which were the shape of lungs, and which were spotted like diseased lungs, that it was intended for the treatment of tuberculosis. Garlic, with it hollow stem, was thought to be a cure for diseases of the windpipe; butter-and-eggs, dandelion, and buttercup, with their yellow flowers, were the jaundice herbs.

In those early times, herbs had important uses in the home. There was no refrigeration; some of the herbs were used for preserving meat. Some were used to repel moths and other insects. Sanitation was unknown; floors were strewn with sweet-smelling herbs, like rosemary, sweet marjoram, thyme. "Strewing" was so universally practiced in England that the "King's Strewing Woman" was an important part of the coronation procession until the year 1685, in which the last "walking coronation" took place—that of James II and Mary of Modena. The Strewing Woman and her maids, carrying gilded baskets lined with satin and filled with herbs, scattered fragrant leaves along the path of the monarch all the way from the Tower to Westminster Abbey.

In those days, the mistress of the house held great responsibility for the health, not only of her family, but of the servants on the place, and for wounded warriors, when the business of life was war. Near the kitchen door she had a planting of herbs for cooking and for the medicines which were concocted in the adjacent "still room." At the end of the growing season the still room shelves were well stocked with ointments and oils, syrups and cordials which were all ready to treat failing appetites and dizziness, war injuries and fevers, and even troubles of the mind and the spirit, which then, as now, were hard to cure.

When peace was upon the land, new and pleasant ways of using the herbs were found. Herbs and flowers were made into fragrant little nosegays called tussie-mussies, and given to friends. These often had hidden meanings, which only those who knew the language of flowers and the symbolism of the herbs could understand. Marjoram meant joy; rosemary, remembrance; myrtle, true love; lemon geranium, unexpected meeting.

*   *   *   *   *

The first herb gardens in Europe were planted in the sixth century by the Benedictine monks at the beautiful monastery of Monte Cassino, which was tragically destroyed in the Second World War. In Italy, in Switzerland, in France, and in England, monks planted herbs in their cloister gardens, and the monasteries became centers of healing. In the security of the cloisters, the monks tended the plants and kept careful records of everything they learned about the use of them. With their herbal medicines, they treated not only their brothers who were ill, but all the people in the villages that lay outside the monastery walls. Within those walls there were two gardens— one which we would call a vegetable garden today, and the other, a physic garden, which held the plants that now grow in our herb gardens. The patients in the nearby infirmary were thought to benefit from the sweet odors blowing in the windows from these medicinal plants.

For nearly a thousand years the quiet study in the monasteries continued, in the ideal conditions of the cloister gardens, but there was no great spreading of knowledge, until printing was brought to England. Then the records of the monks became available, and there was a great wave of interest in herbs and their uses. Gardening books began to appear.

In 1571, Thomas Hyll published *The Gardener's Labyrinth*, which contained gardening information and many designs for gardens. His patterns of interlacing color were designed for planting in gray and green herbs, and were called "knots." The difficulty and expense of their upkeep was the source of much ridicule, to which John Parkinson contributed by describing all the disappointments involved in keeping several different plants in order. His advice was, if one wanted a knot that was simple to maintain, plant it entirely in boxwood. From my own experience,

I know that this advice is just as valid today as it was in the seventeenth century. After struggling two or three years to maintain a knot of assorted santolinas and germander and keep it looking trim and neat, I planted one in boxwood which has been kept in order with very little trouble for fifteen years.

After a long period of popularity, the knot garden in England finally became outmoded, and a new style of French garden design called the parterre took its place. These designs were laid out in complicated scrolls, like embroidery patterns, in sand, or pebbles, or in earth of contrasting colors.

In our great libraries there are fascinating books describing the work of the sixteenth and seventeenth century herbalists, such as Parkinson and Hyll, already mentioned, and Turner, Gerard and Culpeper. The latter was a great figure in London, where he treated his patients in his own hospital. He was an astrologer, who believed that for real efficiency, the herbs needed some help from the stars.

* * * * *

Everywhere that people went, the herbs were taken with them, and so these plants, most of them native to Europe and the shores of the Mediterranean, were brought to America early and planted in the gardens of our forefathers. They have been growing here ever since. Our ancestors had summer savory, dill, sweet marjoram, basil, thyme and sage. Rosemary came, too, because it appears in the famous Josselyn list of herbs growing in New England in 1672. Josselyn said it "did not thrive," which is easy to believe. It must have been a rude transition for any plant from warm Mediterranean shores, which had managed to acclimate itself in Britain, to be subjected to the bitter cold of a New England winter.

* * * * *

Acquaintance with even a few herbs is the beginning of a new experience in gardening. Their fragrance is set free at the slightest touch, and planting is more delightful than it has ever been before. The colors and textures of their leaves are charming, and because of their long history of use and the legends associated with them through the centuries, an herb becomes a bit of human history in one's hand.

You will find that an herb garden invites relaxation. Ideally, it should have the shelter of a roof nearby, some comfortable chairs, and an enclosure of rustic fence, hedge or evergreens. In the heat of the day, in the evening's coolness, or after a summer rain, mingled fragrances drift across the garden and make it a pleasant place to stay.

*   *   *   *   *

A beginner's interest is usually in the kitchen herbs, and indeed, if you want to cook with fresh herbs, you are almost forced to grow your own. Then real adventures in the culinary arts lie ahead.

In Bethlehem, as in most cities, you are limited commercially to parsley, chives, garlic and watercress, with an occasional bunch of dill or leeks appearing in the market, usually at a time when you cannot possibly use it. In New York, Philadelphia, San Francisco or Paris you would have a better selection, but never, never, all the kinds that you want. With herbs in your own garden, you will never feel that your hands are tied for lack of an ingredient. With the simplest kind of herb garden, you will always have on hand the classic *fines herbes*, for a delicious omelet or a salad.

And where, except in your own garden, would you ever find lovage?

*   *   *   *   *

Herbs are bonds between countries and generations. When my first herb garden was new, my mother came for a visit. After dinner, we took her out to see it—just a very small garden of herbs in the form of a V for victory. Suddenly she said, "That plant! Sweet Mary! It was in my mother's garden, and I have not seen it from that day to this." She touched a leaf of costmary,

Bible leaf, mint geranium, alecost, a plant with many names. The name sweet Mary was new to me. A few minutes with my books, however, brought to light this ancient name, and the plant became a bond forever with a grandmother I had never known.

My mother, whose love of plants went back to earliest childhood, told me that as a little girl, walking to school in Eagle, Wisconsin, she passed a pot of musk, covered with yellow flowers. One day, she stopped to smell it, and every day afterward would bury her nose in it, to enjoy a fragrance so wonderful that she could hardly leave it to go on to school. This delightful fragrance made musk a popular house plant in Victorian England. Eleanor Rohde writes that it was trained on six-inch trellises.

Every year I plant that little yellow-flowered *Mimulus moschatus*, and why? Because, during the First World War, all the musk plants all over the world lost their fragrance. It has been called one of the most inexplicable happenings in the whole world of horticulture. Each year I hope that in one of my plants the long-ago fragrance will return, as mysteriously as it disappeared. Perhaps, when we learn to banish war forever from this planet?

* * * * *

Even a seed pod can hold a kind of fascination. The star anise, known in this country only as the lovely brown star which holds the seeds of *Illicium anistatum L.* (and makes a potent cup of tea), is a sacred plant in its native China, and in Japan. Its bark is burned on altars as incense, and branches of it are laid upon altars and upon the graves of friends. Holding the beautiful star, one can only wish to see the evergreen shrub growing and blossoming. The tender star anise plant is rare in America.

It will not be long before the herb gardener discovers the affinity between the herbs and the old roses, especially the everblooming Chinas, Bourbons and noisettes. They belong together. The Bourbon rose, Hermosa (1840) and the China rose

8

called Old Blush are good companions for the herbs. The latter was introduced in England in 1793, but is said on good authority to have been growing in Italy in the early sixteenth century.

In miniature herbal bouquets the comparatively recent polyantha rose, The Fairy (1941), can hold its own with any rose that grows.

Assembling collections of herbs can be wonderful projects. Collecting the thymes could keep one busy and fascinated for years. There are erect thymes, creeping thymes, thymes that love to trail their long blossoming stems over rocks and walls. The *serpyllums* like to be walked on, giving off fragrance at every step. In cool weather, so many leaves of the gold variegated thyme turn bright yellow that the plant looks as though it had burst into bloom. Caraway thyme possesses the true flavor and fragrance of caraway. The variation in leaves, flowers and growth of these plants is an endless enchantment.

Gathering together some of the artemisias would be fun, among them the classic *Artemisia absinthium*. For the most part, this is a gray and white and silver relationship. One exception is the annual sweet mugwort, a tall, soft green feathery plant, with a lovely fragrance and little whirling balls for flowers. It has a way of appearing in the gardens of people who have not planted it, and so delighting them that they will travel a hundred miles to find out what it is. It is the traveler's herb. A sprig in the shoe insures a safe journey.

A collection of sages would be interesting, beginning with the culinary *Salvia officinalis*, with its blue or white flowers. The handsome biennial clary sage, Vatican strain, is a great background plant, with its imposing spikes of rose-colored bracts. The tender perennial pineapple sage is grown for the odor of its foliage, which is intensely redolent of fresh pineapple. In mid-October, just before frost, the tip of every branch bursts into crimson bloom. The perennial Swiss meadow sage bears blue flowers in May, and often thereafter if wilted blossoms are removed. Another perennial, with imposing spires of purple flowers, *Salvia nemorosa*, deserves to be seen more often in herb gardens. One of the prettiest of the sages is the annual *Salvia horminum*. Its striking, colorful bracts, in white, pink or purple, call the attention of the bees to the inconspicuous matching flowers below.

A lovely newcomer in this group of plants is the tender perennial *Salvia dorisiana*, native to Honduras, and first described in 1950. It is a handsome plant with great soft leaves that hold a delightful fragrance which is described differently by everyone who smells it. Potted cuttings make pleasant house plants. When planted in the garden in the spring, it does its best to take over. Except that it doesn't climb, it grows like Jack's beanstalk, so it must be given plenty of room to grow to four or five feet in height and about three feet in diameter.

One of the great collectors is Miss Edna K. Neugebauer, of Pasadena, California. In 1948, she was obliged to stay at home because of family responsibilities, and spent much time in her herb garden. Becoming interested in the lavenders, she began to collect them, and although she could not leave Pasadena, she traveled by correspondence to twenty-three countries on five continents in her quest. I remember her comparison of two of her discoveries—a tiny lavender about three inches tall, and a great Dutch lavender which reached a height of three feet. Once when a young man of her acquaintance wrote his doctoral thesis on the lavenders, she was able to give him twenty-two plants for his collection.

*   *   *   *   *

An herb garden can be a wonderful, cloistered retreat, but I like to think of it, too, as a garden from which many paths lead out—out into the world.

With a little knowledge of herbs, literature with herbal references takes on new meaning; ancient tapestries acquire new beauty; the lovely mille-fleur backgrounds become hunting grounds for herbs. There, and in the main design of the tapestry, one searches for herbs and studies their symbolism.

Seeking original sources for legends and uses of herbs leads first to old manuscripts and then to old books, and to a new appreciation of prints, bindings, and first editions. Shall I ever forget that day in the British Museum when I held in my hands the oldest Saxon book, the *Leech Book of Bald?* Written in the year 900, it was as fresh and clean as though it had just come from the hand of the scribe.

On the same day, I saw the famous so-called letter written by Jeanne de Valois, Countess of Hainaut, in France, to her daughter Queen Philippa of England, wife of Edward III. Written in English, it is more like a book than a letter. The first part is a treatise on the medicinal herbs, and the last part extols the virtues of the great herb rosemary. It contains stories and legends not found elsewhere. The date of this epistle is 1338.

A study of the use of herbs in other countries leads to an understanding of other civilizations than our own. The history of herbs is also tied up with archaeological exploration and that field lies at the end of another path.

These are some of the paths leading out of an herb garden, and at the end of each path one finds new friends.

Innumerable pleasures, countless rewards, come from growing, studying and using the herbs, but there is none greater than the friendships that one makes along the way.

A BEGINNER'S HERB GARDEN
(4' x 7')

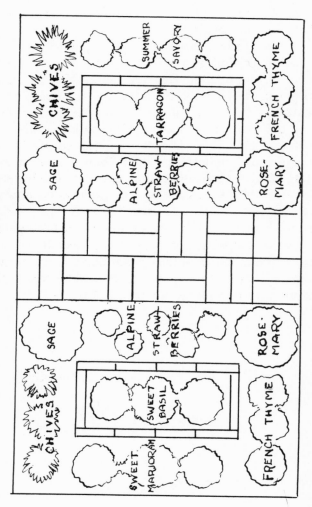

This design contains only nine of the twelve herbs in the Beginner's Herb Garden list. The reason for these omissions is that this is a garden in the open sunshine, and the three missing herbs all like shade, in varying degrees. Sweet woodruff likes deep shade, as in a woods; chervil enjoys living under taller plants, which offer some protection from the sun. Spearmint will tolerate considerable sun, but is such a rampant plant that it should never be planted in a garden which makes any claim to having a design. It will overrun everything. I have had no success in trying to keep it contained with bricks, underground.

Look around your garden. Hopefully, you may find just the places for these three plants.

II

THE BEGINNER'S HERB GARDEN

The growing of a first few herbs is the discovery of a whole new world of garden pleasure and human meaning, but it is when a gardener has tried a few, liked them and been liked by them, and would go on, that the full adventure begins.

Henry Beston, *Herbs and the Earth*

If you were to ask ten herb gardeners for a list of twelve basic culinary herbs, there would certainly be some variation in their selections, but I think that at least eight of the plants on my list would be found on every list. You will notice that I have not included parsley in this basic list, important as it is. Everyone has parsley—even apartment dwellers have little patches which they harvest and put in the freezer.

These herbs are essential in cookery; they are easy to grow, and you can begin to use some of them almost at once. Then the fun begins.

This is my Beginner's List:
Hardy Perennials
Alpine Strawberry   *Fragaria vesca* var. *Alexandria*
Chives   *Allium schoenoprasum*
Sage   *Salvia officinalis*
Spearmint   *Mentha spicata* var. *viridis*
Sweet Woodruff   *Asperula odorata*
Tarragon   *Artemisia dracunculus* var. *sativus*
Thyme   *Thymus vulgaris* var. narrow-leaved French

Tender Perennial
Rosemary   *Rosmarinus officinalis*

Biennial
Chervil *Anthriscus cerefolium*

Annuals
Summer Savory *Satureja hortensis*
Sweet Basil *Ocimum basilicum*
Sweet Marjoram *Origanum majorana*
>   (Sweet Marjoram is really a tender perennial, but in cold
>   climates is always treated as an annual. It will not survive
>   a Pennsylvania winter even in a cold frame.)

In this design for a small new herb garden, only nine of the
twelve herbs in the Beginner's Herb Garden list appear. This is
because chervil and sweet woodruff must have shade, and
because spearmint must never be planted in a bed with other
herbs. Nice as it is to have and to use, it is too invasive to plant in
a patterned bed. Find a shady spot for the sweet woodruff, and
the chervil, and a place for spearmint where it will have room to
spread. A shaded spot will do, but it does not like the deep shade
in which sweet woodruff thrives. Chervil is content to grow in the
shade of taller plants.

All of these plants will thrive in good, well-drained garden soil.
Spearmint likes some shade, as does chervil. Tarragon tolerates a
little shade, and sweet woodruff must have it. Indeed, it grows
best in woods, under trees. All the others enjoy full sun.

ALPINE STRAWBERRY *Fragaria vesca* var. Alexandria

Alpine strawberries are everbearing plants, which display
flowers and fruit all through the summer, from June until a hard
frost. Because they form no runners, the plants remain symmetrical, and the berries are often held high above the foliage. They
make a pretty border for a garden of herbs.

When well grown, in rich soil in full sun, they are larger than
our native wild strawberries, and they taste good. The flavor is

not equal to that of the best, cultivated large berries, but they are delightful used in the ways mentioned here.

The Alpine strawberry is easily grown from seed, but while seed planted early in a greenhouse, or outdoors in April, will produce strong plants by fall, there will be no flowers nor fruit that year. Plants, set out in April, will blossom and bear fruit at once, hopefully in time to decorate the *mai bowle*, which is their most delightful use today. The berries are always a pretty addition to fruit cups, and to midwinter strawberry omelets.

Since these plants form no runners, they should be separated and re-set every two or three years, replacements, if necessary, being made from the seedlings which spring up around established plants. The addition of rotted manure and compost to the soil will improve the size and quality of the berries. They need plenty of moisture and room to grow. In a year or two, you will have plants to give away to your friends.

A seedling, potted in September, and taken into the house before frost, will blossom and bear fruit all winter in a sunny window.

The Harvest

Leaves for tea can be picked all through the summer, choosing the finest ones; the berries should be picked every two or three days, and frozen in small plastic envelopes. Keep these envelopes in a large container in the freezer. It is then easy to take out just the number of packages you need.

CHIVES   Allium schoenoprasum

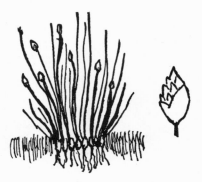

Next to parsley and spearmint, chives is probably the best known herb. Tasting delicately of onion, it is indispensable in the kitchen. My first memory of chives goes back to early childhood in Philadelphia, when François Supiot, who brought green things to my mother every week from his wonderful garden, introduced her to chives. He recommended cutting it very fine and adding it to cottage cheese, with sugar, sour cream and a little salt. It has been used in this way in our family ever since.

One of the first herbs to make its appearance in the spring, the plants will grow almost anywhere in the sun. In May, a row of chives in bloom is a pretty sight. Enjoy the blossoms for a week or two, and then cut each blossoming spear individually down to the ground. This is a tedious operation, but it is necessary because the flowering stems are stiff and inedible, and if they are not removed, you will have to separate them from the edible spears all summer.

This pruning operation is not entirely without its reward, because a good chives blossom vinegar can be made from these discarded stems and flowers.

Chives comes easily from seed, but it is so easy to find clumps ready to plant in the spring that it is hardly worth waiting for the seed to come up. A clump can be divided so that one pot of chives will provide a good many plants.

Mature clumps should be divided and re-set every two or three years. If a pot of chives is wanted on a kitchen windowsill during the winter, plant some bulbs in a pot in late summer and sink it into the ground. After frost comes, cover it with salt hay or put it in a cold frame, and leave it outdoors for three months. Brought into the house, to warmth, sunshine and watering, in January, the green shoots will soon appear. Chives must have this rest period.

The green spears of chives should always be cut very fine with sharp scissors, for any use at all. Long pieces are unappetizing.

The Harvest

The best time to cut the amount of chives needed for the winter is right after the blossoms have been removed. Wash, drain, and cut them up very fine. Fill a glass or a plastic container, and put it into the freezer. Even when chives are frozen hard, you can separate the amount needed, using a strong knife.

For this herb, freezing is a great boon. The dried herb loses much of its flavor, though it can be used in this way if no freezing facilities are available. The frozen product is so good that it is almost as satisfactory as the fresh.

SAGE   Salvia officinalis

Sage is a familiar, gray-leaved strongly-scented plant which has been known from antiquity when it was highly regarded as a medicinal herb. It is still one of the most popular seasoning herbs, all over the world, used to flavor meat, cheese, poultry

17

stuffing and bread. Begin by buying plants; sage can be increased readily from cuttings. Because of the tendency of the plants to become woody, a judicious pruning of the old branches is advisable every spring.

The Harvest

Sage plants are so pretty when in bloom, some with blue flowers, some with white, that I wait until the blossoms have wilted to harvest the crop. First, cut off each blossoming stem at ground level, saving the leaves on it, and some woody stems for the fireplace. Then take about half of each remaining stem to dry. There will be a fine growth of leaves at this time, and if the plant grows back luxuriantly, it will be possible to take another cutting in early September. It must not be cut back severely at this time, however, or there will not be enough foliage left to insure its surviving the winter.

Sage tastes better dried than fresh, and is so pleasant to use that way that I have never considered freezing it.

SPEARMINT *Mentha spicata* var. *viridis*

If there can be just one mint in the garden, let that one be spearmint. Start with plants, or beg a rooted runner from a friend. Spearmint will live almost anywhere, but thrives best in a moist, somewhat shaded situation—near a dripping faucet, or close to the overflow of a lily pool. The mints grow best around pools as they did in the old monastery gardens. Spearmint spreads so rapidly that it is almost impossible to keep it within bounds. Even when the roots are surrounded by bricks, underground, the runners will escape and have to be trimmed. Plant it in its own corner, if possible, where it can run rampant, and not interfere with other plantings.

The spearmint bed should be dug up and re-set every two or three years, and at that time it should have a top dressing of manure or good compost. This is also advisable after harvesting the crop.

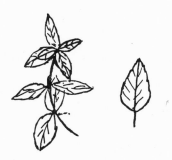

The Harvest

Cut the first crop just as the flower buds are beginning to open, taking about half of each stem. A second crop can usually be cut in early September.

SWEET WOODRUFF *Asperula odorata*

One of the most delightful of the herbs, sweet woodruff is a low-growing plant, about six inches high, with pretty star-like whorls of leaves. The plants are covered with pure white, four-petaled flowers in May. It was of minor importance in medicine, and was never a pot-herb, but because of its lovely fragrance, it was an important strewing herb. Its odor is always likened to the smell of new-mown hay, and is intensified by drying. Actually there is a basis for this comparison, because both hay and sweet woodruff contain coumarin.

Sweet woodruff is a shade-loving plant, and flourishes under trees in a pine woods, where it quite justifies its German name of *waldmeister* by taking over the woods. It does this in a pleasant way, because there are never any weeds among the plants, and it makes a beautiful ground cover for a moist, shady situation with no attention at all. You will always be able to supply your friends with rooted runners.

The Harvest

Pick the leaves for drying soon after the plants have finished blooming. There is never any reason to freeze this herb, except as decoration in an ice ring.

TARRAGON *Artemisia dracunculus* var. *sativus*

Tarragon is one of the aristocrats of the herb garden, and indispensable in the kitchen. A native of Siberia, it is extremely hardy, and has been so widely cultivated and used in France that it is known as French tarragon. The true French tarragon almost never blooms and absolutely never sets seed, so that it must be propagated by root divisions or cuttings. Seed is sometimes offered, even by reputable seed houses, but beware of it; the plants, of so-called Russian tarragon, will be as tasteless as grass.

Tarragon likes a rich, very sandy soil, in a well drained situation. Two or three plants will be enough to start, for they increase even in one year. Each spring the plants should be divided and re-planted, and every third year the whole bed should be dug up and changed to a new location. When well grown, tarragon will be two feet or more in height.

Tarragon has always been chiefly a kitchen herb, best known as the flavoring for tarragon vinegar, an essential ingredient in *Sauce tartare*. It is one of the best salad herbs.

The Harvest

Choose a hot day in mid-July, and cut half of every stem. If the plants are growing well, it may be possible to take another crop in early September.

21

THYME *Thymus vulgaris* var. *narrow-leaved French*

The thymes are native plants of the rocky outcrops along the Mediterranean coast from Italy to Portugal. They are also found, in a wild state, on dry, chalky downs and exposed cliffs, all over England.

Although all the thymes have pleasant aromas and interesting flavors, we are especially concerned here with the graygreen narrow-leaved French variety, which has the best flavor for use in cooking. An erect little plant about ten inches tall, it makes a pretty border or a small hedge, and likes to grow in friable, alkaline, gritty soil with good drainage. A damp spot can be fatal. Start with plants of French thyme. Plants are easy to find, and cuttings take root readily, so that one's stock may easily be increased. Although it is hardy, it is well to protect it, especially from the north and the east in places where the winter is as cold as in Bethlehem, Pennsylvania. Surround the plants with salt hay or oak leaves. If a cold frame is available that is still better. Cuttings taken in August and placed in the cold frame will be sturdy little plants by spring.

The Harvest

Shear the plants right after they bloom, and dry them. Dried thyme is easier to use in winter than the frozen herb, and the flavor is so good that I have never frozen it since the first experiment.

ROSEMARY *Rosmarinus officinalis*

Even the smallest herb garden would be incomplete without a plant or two of rosemary, one of the most fragrant of all herbs. Its aromatic leaves smell strongly of pine and spice, and the odor is stimulating and refreshing and universally liked.

It is best to buy plants, as raising it from seed is slow. Propagation is by cuttings, which root easily, and by layering. Rosemary likes a sunny situation in well-drained soil, with plenty of room to grow. A handful of powdered limestone should be dug in around the plants several times a year, and some dried cow manure occasionally. It is a woody shrub which reaches six feet in height in the mild climate of its native Mediterranean countries.

Rosemary is tender north of Washington, D.C., but it will take only a brief acquaintance with the charms of this herb to understand why northern herb growers go to such lengths to protect it in the winter. The plant can be potted in late summer, early enough to have time to become accustomed to the pot before having to adapt to the atmosphere of the house. Placed in a sunny window, in a saucer of pebbles holding water which does not touch the bottom of the pot, rosemary will usually thrive, if the plant is kept moist and if the leaves are sprayed with lukewarm water occasionally. However, in spite of one's best efforts, once in a while a plant will dry up and die, for no apparent reason.

A rosemary plant potted and taken into a greenhouse in the fall will thrive, and that is the way I kept mine, enjoying the top light, for many years. However, a plant so treated never attains the height and breadth of one that stays in one place outdoors all the year.

My first attempt at keeping one outdoors was planting a sturdy rosemary in the angle formed by the south wall of the house and the glass wall of the greenhouse. The morning after I did this, I found a note from my husband at my place on the breakfast table, informing me in legal terms that if the rosemary was going to occupy the most protected situation on our place, it would have to pay rent, and the rent was one blossom by the fifteenth of March every year. The twinkle in his eyes belied the formal language of the document.

That plant managed to live, and to pay the rent, but it looked so sad and bedraggled by spring that I knew I had to give it more protection.

Then my husband built a kind of shelter on the south side of the unheated herb house. It was just a wooden frame covered with plastic, with a lid that could be raised. This he called the rosemarium, and it was a great success. The plants bloomed in that enclosure, and the fragrance, when the lid was lifted, was overwhelming.

Then I tried another way that proved successful. I had a pit dug, deep enough to hold the potted plants below the frost line, and covered the pit with glass. On a mild day in winter, the glass was removed; the plants were watered and allowed to enjoy unfiltered sunshine for a while. They bloomed in the pit and were off to a good start when they were set out in the spring.

For the last eight years, my big rosemarys have lived outdoors with a different kind of protection. Planted along the south wall of the house, I have had old, discarded storm windows built up around them. As the plants grow larger, we have had to increase the size of the covering, and this has been done, when we ran out of windows, with plastic-covered wire screening. It seems that one thickness of glass or plastic is all the protection a rosemary plant needs from the cold of a Pennsylvania winter. Our temperatures in Bethlehem sometimes, but not often, go down to several degrees below zero, the lowest ever recorded being 12 degrees below zero.

These plants do not get direct sunshine, because they are

partly shaded by the house next door. The plant with the best exposure attained a height of five feet by last spring, and it was five feet in diameter—really comparable to some that I have seen in California.

This covering is not a great deal of trouble, for it takes a man less than half a day to construct it. It is really quite a makeshift arrangement, because it is by no means air or water tight. Perhaps that is just as well, because the plants do have ventilation, and they certainly get some water from rain and melting snow.

However, it could be much more trouble than this, and I would still think it worthwhile. It is thrilling to me to look through the windows of my basement art gallery, and see great rosemary plants, completely green and, in early spring, in bloom, white flowered at one end, dark blue at the other. By opening the windows, I can water them when they need it; I can pick some rosemary for a bride's bouquet, or to put in a letter, or in the vegetable soup, with no trouble at all. Even non-herb growers enjoy these plants, especially on a winter day, when they stand, green and flourishing, against the background of a freezing, snow-covered world.

The Harvest

Fresh rosemary tastes better than dried. One of the advantages of having a pot of rosemary indoors is that you may pick some fresh at any time. It is good frozen, too. Cut it fine with sharp scissors before freezing it. If you dry it, crumble it fine before putting it into air-tight jars. Pick it at any time.

CHERVIL   *Anthriscus cerefolium*

Plant seeds outdoors in March or early April, underneath taller plants. Chervil likes shade, and thrives in this protection. It is a pretty, delicate herb, somewhat resembling parsley, but with much softer, fernlike leaves and an entirely different flavor like a mild anise. The plants will reach a height of about twelve inches in the garden, and will bloom the first year, self-sowing generously. If seedlings are lifted in late summer and put in a cold frame, they will survive the winter there, and in the spring, when the glass is removed, will shoot up to a height of thirty inches, cover themselves with blossoms, and die. Grown in this way, fresh leaves can be had all the year, and plenty of seed.

26

Chervil is dainty and feathery, and a pretty garnish. If it is to be so used, it should be picked early in the morning of the day needed, and kept in water in the refrigerator to harden. Then it will do honor to any platter. It is a good salad herb, and is a favorite herb in France, especially in egg dishes. *"Aux fines herbes"* usually means chives, chervil and parsley.

SUMMER SAVORY *Satureja hortensis*

Summer savory is a symmetrical little annual about eighteen inches tall, a pretty plant from the time it blooms until after it has gone to seed.

For fresh leaves all summer and plenty of flowers for little bouquets, a succession of plantings, at least two, should be made, beginning in very early spring. Its pleasant, peppery, "herby" taste makes it an indispensable herb in the kitchen, and it is impossible to have too much, because little jars of the dried herb always make welcome gifts.

Summer savory self-sows generously. I always transplant the volunteer seedlings into locations of my choice, but I buy fresh seed every year, to insure having enough.

This herb likes good soil, made friable with sand and compost, and enjoys a situation in full sunshine.

27

The Harvest

When the plants are in bloom, pull them up and hang them by their roots to dry. If the drying location is not as dust-free as an attic, each plant should be put into a paper bag, top down. Tie roots and bag together, and hang on hooks.

Summer savory is good frozen, but it has such excellent flavor when dried that I have not frozen it again since my first experiment.

SWEET BASIL *Ocimum basilicum*

There are many varieties of basil, in both green-leaved and purple-leaved forms. The most charming one of all, the dwarf purple basil has, alas, disappeared from the scene, and I eagerly await the day when some botanist will have both the time and the interest to develop it again. Grief at its loss has been somewhat mitigated by the appearance of the lovely Dark Opal Basil which, so far, the seed growers have kept true to color and form. There are lettuce-leaved and lemon-scented basils, and dwarf bush basils, and they are all delightfully fragrant except the holy basil of India, which few people find pleasant. They are all tender annuals, which turn black at the first touch of frost. The only one which self-sows is the holy basil. All the others have good and varying flavors, but sweet basil remains the classic culinary basil, an absolutely indispensable herb. It grows quickly from seed, which germinates in five days. The seedlings should be transplanted to stand ten inches apart. It likes full sun.

The Harvest

Cut the tips of all the stems when flower buds begin to form, in the hope of a good second growth. At the second harvest, pull up the entire plant and dry like summer savory.

Sweet basil tastes so good dried that I freeze only a small part of the harvest. Even when carefully dried, however, some of the leaves turn a little brown. The color of the frozen herb is not perfect either, but the flavor of both is excellent.

SWEET MARJORAM   *Origanum majorana*

Sweet majoram is one of the most valuable kitchen herbs. For seasoning, it combines well with thyme, sage, and summer savory. It is an intensely fragrant little plant, a native of Portugal, which grows from six to ten inches tall. Seed should be planted indoors in early April, and the seedlings set out in late May. To treat it like an annual is the only way to grow it in a climate as cold as this part of Pennsylvania.

The plant likes an alkaline soil, light, sandy, and well-drained, and a sunny situation. Like most of the herbs, it is easily grown, and submits to drought or deluge without complaint.

The Harvest

When the plants begin to show flower buds, cut off a little less than half of each stem, and by late summer there will be a second crop, when the whole plant should be pulled up. It is good frozen, but so very satisfactory dried that I dry the whole crop.

* * * * *

Through centuries of association with man, each of the plants in the Beginner's Herb Garden, like every other herb, has acquired a store of legends, folk-lore, and medicinal uses which cling to it like a garment. This is always interesting to the people who watch the plants grow in their gardens, so I am going to record some of them. After reading their stories, you may feel like the herbalist of old, who said, of the lore in his own manuscript, "Most of which I am confident are true, but if there be any that are not so, at least they are pleasant."

STRAWBERRY

This old herb, a native wild plant of Europe, was grown in the sixteenth century for a long list of medicinal uses, both the berries and an infusion of the leaves being used. The former were recommended for the treatment of gout, and the latter for jaundice, palpitation of the heart, and to fasten loose teeth!

A tea made from the leaves was used as a cosmetic, and was also enjoyed as a beverage, alone, and in combination with other herbs, lemon balm, sweet woodruff or lemon verbena.

A well-liked mixture was made of equal quantities of sweet woodruff and strawberry leaves. Dethicke points out "such innocency of this herb, . . . which . . . hath no affinity with poyson." Coles advises (1656), "Among strawberries plant here and there some borage seed, and you shall find the strawberries under those leaves farre more larger than their fellowes."

30

Tusser writes (1580):

Wife, unto thy garden and set me a plot
With strawberry roots, the best to be got
Such growing abroad amongst thorns in the wood,
Well chosen and picked, prove excellent food.

Until the nineteenth century, our present garden strawberry was unknown. This was an old London street cry:

Rare, ripe strawberries and
Haût-boys sixpence a pottle
Full to the bottom haût-boys!
Strawberries and cream are charming and sweet
Mix them and see how delightful they eat.

(On page 528 of the 1656 edition of Paradisi in Sole in the Hunt Library, there is a handwritten note which says that the haût-boy was a Bohemian strawberry.)

Strawberry leaves decorate the coronets of the British nobility, and because the duke's coronet boasts more leaves than any other, the term "strawberry leaves" has come to mean a dukedom.

The plant acquired, also, a Christian symbolism. In medieval paintings, the Virgin's dress would be decorated with strawberry leaves, signifying the fruit of the spirit, the good works of the righteous. Renaissance doctors talked of the strawberry as a cure for "passions of the heart," and for "reviving low spirits," and "making the heart merry."

SAGE

The very name is derived from the Latin *salvere*, "to be well," which refers to the curative properties of the plant.

Cur moriatur homo cui Salvia crescit in horto? (Why should a man die while sage grows in his garden?)

The old saying that "He who drinks of sage in May will live for aye" was taken seriously by European peasants who not only drank sage tea, but made a serious business of spreading fresh sage leaves on their buttered bread all through the month of May.

The herb has always been used as much to prevent disease as to restore health.

Sir John Hill writes at length about the virtues of sage in lengthening human life. He calls it "a gentle stimulus, a mild and temperate balsam, a cordial and a sedative."

Aetius, a distinguished Greek physician of the sixth century A.D., author of a medical work of sixteen books, held sage in high regard, and pronounced it "friendly to conception." He also said that disorders of the head and nerves were cured by it.

Simon Pauli, an anatomist of the sixteenth century, reported that "live palsy" was cured by sage. Similar claims are reported from other sources.

A story is told of a woman in a little town near Peterborough. She lived on five square yards of ground planted in sage, which constituted a large part of her diet. She lived to be so old that she was thought to be a witch.

In nearby Peterborough Cathedral, the sexton lived so long that he "buried all the inhabitants of the town twice over." Near the bench where he slept grew some ancient plants of sage, which he used exclusively for his beverage.

The leaves of the plant were used in all these instances, but the roots and the seeds were believed to have great power.

Sage tea had another use in Bethlehem, Pennsylvania. I am told that, two generations back, there were no gray-haired ladies in the town. The sight of one gray hair was the signal for the appearance of a bowl of strong sage tea on the lady's dressing table. At night, a hair brush was dipped into the tea, and the offending gray was assiduously brushed away. A Bethlehem hairdresser who knows of this custom admits that it really worked. Sage was for brunettes, he says. Chamomile was for blondes.

Since colonial days in America sage tea has been considered a reliable remedy for colds. The Chinese were so fond of sage tea that at one time they exchanged four pounds of their best tea for one pound of dried sage leaves.

SPEARMINT

This fragrant herb has been known and used since ancient times. It was one of the strewing herbs and was used to perfume baths.

Bundles of it used to be packed with grains, to keep rodents away. Mice are said to detest the odor of spearmint, both fresh and dried, and will avoid any food near it.

Gerard says that "the smell rejoiceth the heart of man, for which cause they used to strew it in chambers and places of recreation, pleasure and repose, where feasts and banquets are made." He goes on to recommend it for "watering eyes and all manner of sores," for the "biting of mad dogs," and "the stinging of wasps and bees."

Spearmint was established in New England early; the seeds may have crossed the Atlantic in the pockets of the women on the *Mayflower*, and other ships, for it appears on Josselyn's list.

The plant still retains some medicinal uses, but today it is primarily a culinary herb. It is useful as a tea in its own right, or in a mixture with sweet woodruff. A delicious mixture is made of equal parts of dried spearmint and orange pekoe. It is a cooling herb in summer and flavors iced drinks, jelly, vinegar, and a sauce for roast lamb. The latter not only tastes delicious, but is said to be a real aid to digestion.

SWEET WOODRUFF

The plant is native to the dark, shady forests of Asia and Europe, and first appears in Saxon leechbooks in the year 1000 A.D. as "wuderofe," in smelling salts for headaches.

In the fourteenth century it was used in England and in Sweden in an ointment called "Herb Walter," for Walter de

Elvesdon, of whom nothing is known. The name was soon contracted to "herb water."

An item appears among the warden's accounts in a London church during the reign of Edward IV (1442-1483): "For rose garlondis and woodrove garlondis on St. Barnabas Day (June 11th) 11 pence."

Sprigs were taken to church with sweet Mary and other aromatic leaves, and were also laid between the pages of books. Sweet woodruff was used, too, as a moth preventive, and one writer said there was "a sweet breath of cowslips" when bureau drawers containing sweet woodruff were opened. The old French name was *muge des bois* (musk of the woods).

German references to sweet woodruff occur as early as 1265, and indeed the plant has been used to flavor May wine in Germany for centuries. The *Mai Bowle* is served on May Day, and thereafter during the month of May. German sections of American cities can be identified in the spring by the advertisements of May wine appearing in store windows and on the menus in restaurants.

The old-fashioned recipes for May wine, containing white wine, brandy and champagne, have never appealed to me as much as a simpler product made by steeping sweet woodruff in a good white wine of your own choice. However, it has been possible during the last few years to buy such an excellent May wine, every spring, that I do not make it any more, but confine my efforts to making an ice ring to chill the bowl from sweet woodruff with its blossoms, and Alpine strawberries. In my house, you are likely to have May wine at any time through June, July and August.

A good punch is made from a base of dried sweet woodruff tea. This herb gives a delicious flavor to beverages, an indefinable, delectable taste, which only the initiated can identify.

THYME

This is an herb that has been important for two thousand years, in medicine, as an allure for bees, as forage for sheep, in perfume making, and as an essential seasoning in cookery.

Poets have sung its praises; Horace pays tribute to thyme in his Odes and Epistles; Vergil mentions "bees feasting on thyme" in Eclogue V, and refers to it in other Eclogues and in the Georgics. Thyme was one of the three herbs which lined the holy manger in Bethlehem of Judea. Hippocrates used oil of thyme rubbed on the forehead for treating headaches, insomnia and fainting spells. As a tea, it was used for colds and infections. Centuries later, Sir John Hill reported that nightmares were "perfectly cured" by drinking thyme tea. The oil has always been used to disguise disagreeable odors and tastes in medicine.

In the third century, Theocritus wrote of

Thick-growing thyme, and roses wet with dew
Sacred to the sisterhood divine of Helicon.

Thyme-covered fields have always been favored grazing grounds for sheep. A diet of thyme is thought to improve the flavor of roast lamb.

The pleasing aromatic scent of thyme made it one of the chief strewing herbs, and it was spread upon the floors of monasteries and churches and ceremonial halls. In "The Prelude," Wordsworth writes,

And now his feet crush out a livelier fragrance
    from the flowers of lowly thyme
By nature's skill enwrought in the wild turf.

In the eighteenth century, the temptation to make puns was as strong as it is today, because William Shenstone wrote of "pun-provoking thyme."

In *Two Noble Kinsmen*, a play by John Fletcher and William Shakespeare, is found the following:

Maiden pinks of odor faint
Daisies smell-less, yet more quaint
And sweet thyme true.

By the twelfth century thyme was a recognized pot herb in England, and Izaak Walton mentions it as a seasoning for fish sauces and stuffings.

The delicious flavor of honey from the hives of bees that "feast on thyme" has been appreciated ever since there have been thyme and bees. The favorite of the ancient world was the honey from the thyme-clad hills of Mt. Hybla, in Sicily, but first place has been given during the last centuries to the honey from Mt. Hymettus in Greece. This honey is available in this country, and perhaps they export the best of the crop, because I have tasted Mt. Hymettus honey which was bought in Greece. It was merely good, while that which is found in specialty shops here is supreme.

Dr. John Armstrong, a controversial English physician who was more interested in writing than in practicing medicine, published, in 1744, a poem called "The Art of Preserving Health." In it he expresses his opinion that the land on which thyme naturally grows is especially healthful for human habitation.

> . . . where marjoram and thyme,
> the love of bees, perfume the air
> There build thy roofs; high on the basking steep
> Ascend; there light thy hospitable fires.

ROSEMARY

Christmas legends cling to this herb. When the Holy Family sought shelter on the flight into Egypt, the branches of the bushes through which they passed crackled, making their progress audible. Only the rosemary stretched out its branches in silence, and let them pass safely through.

Another familiar legend is that the Virgin threw her cloak on a rosemary bush, and the flowers, white before, turned blue, the color of her cloak.

When Mary hung the Christ Child's clothing on a rosemary bush, she found she had hung it on a sunbeam, and after that the plant was endowed with magical power.

Through the ages, rosemary has been beloved by people everywhere for ever-increasing reasons. Herb of remembrance, sacred to friendship, "a sprig of it hath a dumb language." A child-like belief in its magic still persists. No wonder it has travelled all over the world.

It grew in Egyptian wall gardens, travelled to Britain with the Romans, and became acclimated there. It is probably as much at home in Southern England as on its native Mediterranean shores from which Sir Francis Bacon said you could smell the fragrance on a ship twenty miles at sea.

Magical, almost holy properties have been attributed to this herb. It was believed to strengthen the memory, the brain and the heart. A symbol of fidelity and devotion, it was used not only at weddings, but also at funerals. With bay and mistletoe, it was part of the Christmas decorations.

A tea made of the leaves and flowers was said to restore a failing appetite and cure the gout. To smell a box made of rosemary wood preserved youth, and a branch under the bed warded off all evil spirits.

SUMMER SAVORY

Summer savory has always been, first of all, a kitchen herb, but Culpeper does record using the juice of the plant, dropped in the eyes, "to remove dimness of sight." The same juice, mixed with oil of roses, dropped in the ears, cured deafness. He gave the herb credit for quickening dull spirits, and easing sciatica. The leaves, when rubbed on a bee sting, gave instant relief. So it was not without honorable mention in medicine.

The herb was described by Pliny and Vergil called it one of the most fragrant of all the herbs.

Shakespeare refers to it, with the mints, marjoram and lavender, in *The Winter's Tale.*

It is included in Josselyn's famous list of herbs growing in New England in the seventeenth century.

BASIL

Basil is so essential a seasoning in Italian dishes that a pot of basil on the back porch of an apartment is a common sight in the Italian sections of big cities, and I have seen such pots of basil in Bethlehem. Deprived of any space for a garden, basil is the one fresh seasoning an Italian family cannot do without.

Superstition and folk lore surround this herb. In India, the sacred basil *Ocimum sanctum* is a holy plant, and a charm against any and all calamities. An old legend explains the sanctity of this Indian basil, or tulsi. Tulasi, the wife of the god Vishnu, returned to earth in the form of this simple herb. Therefore the plant, to the Indian, represents the goddess.

An Indian student at Lehigh University told me that his father keeps a pot of basil at the front door of his house. Each morning he picks a sprig, dips it in his bath water, sprinkles himself with it, and then pours some of the bath water on the plant. This ceremony provides protection from all evil for the whole day.

Both Greeks and Romans believed that basil and rue will not grow together, and that basil will not grow unless the planter curses violently when he places the seed in the ground. From this belief has grown the French expression *semer le basilic*, meaning to slander or abuse.

In Italy, a pot of basil in the window tells a lover that his lady is expecting him. Isabella, in Keats's poem, kept the head of her lover in a pot of basil.

Basil is an important herb in Bethlehem. Father Negrepontis of the Greek Orthodox Church told me that all Greeks love basil, but especially those Greeks who live on the island of Crete. Each year he imports basil seed from Greece, and it is planted by the members of his congregation.

He told a story of St. Helen, mother of Constantine the Great, who lived early in the fourth century and made a pilgrimage in search of the Holy Cross. The church owns a manuscript describing her journey to Golgotha with her company. They found three crosses, and on one of them grew a basil plant. That was designated the true Cross, and pieces of that Cross are still treasured in Greek families.

Every year, on September fourteenth, the day of the celebration of the Holy Cross, his parishioners bring whole plants of basil from their gardens. The priest carries a basket of basil and goes around the church, singing. At other times, he blesses their homes with basil, and the plant has a place in many religious ceremonies.

Oddly enough, basil has never been much used in medicine. Dioscorides does tell of some long-ago medicinal benefits, but they were not important, and they have been completely obscured by other uses of the plant which have continued right down to the present day.

SWEET MARJORAM

Sweet marjoram has been known and used so long that it is rich in legends, and is said to have been originated by Venus.

One day, while Venus was romping in her garden with Cupid, one of his love darts struck her arm. Looking around quickly for a remedy, she found no herb potent enough to be effective against a love dart, and she commanded sweet marjoram to spring up to help her. In her haste, she gave the plant the wrong power, and her wound was made worse instead of better. Holding a sweet marjoram leaf in her hand, she saw Adonis, and straightway fell in love. Great power as a love charm has been attributed to this herb, and the Greeks and Romans crowned young married couples with it.

One Greek myth concerns a young page in the palace of the King of Cyprus. Carrying a vase filled with precious perfume, he fell, shattering it. Terrified, he swooned into the pool of perfume, and the gods changed him into a fragrant sweet marjoram plant.

Sweet marjoram is planted on graves in Greece, to assure the rest of the loved ones lying there.

Esther Singleton writes that it was a well-loved potted plant in English cottage windows, and was used in a sweet washing water.

In the *Aeneid* (I:693-4) Vergil writes "where the sweet marjoram, breathing its fragrance, surrounds him with flowers and soft shade." An old name for it was "joy of the mountain."

It was a great favorite of our forefathers, who called it "knotted marjoram." because of the tight little flower heads.

In France, the fragrant sprigs were tucked away with keepsakes, but it was also added to the salad.

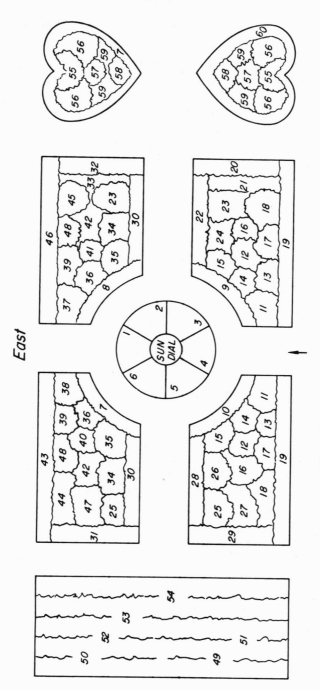

East

The Expanding Herb Garden

KEY TO THE EXPANDING HERB GARDEN

1. Wooly thyme *Thymus serpyllum lanuginosus*
2. Gold thyme *T. serpyllum aureus*
3. White-flowered creeping thyme *T. serpyllum albus*
4. Crimson-flavored creeping thyme *T. serpyllum coccineus*
5. Gold variegated thyme *T. serpyllum variegatus*
6. Caraway scented thyme *T. herba barona*
7. Pink-flowered thrift *Armeria maritima*
8. Roof houseleek *Sempervivum tectorum*
9. Winter savory *Satureja montana*
10. Pineapple mint *Mentha rotundifolia variegata*
11. Sweet bay *Laurus nobilis*
12. Madonna lilies *Lilium candidum*
13. Crown imperial *Fritillaria imperialis*
14. Lemon balm *Melissa officinalis*
15. Burnet *Sanguisorba officinalis*
16. Angelica *Angelica archangelica*
17. French sorrel *Rumex scutatus*
18. Tarragon *Artemisia dracunculus* var. *sativa*
19. English boxwood *Buxus sempervirens*
20. Pink-flowered hyssop *Hyssopus officinalis ruber*
21. Salvia horminum, pink-flowered *Salvia horminum* Pink Sundae
22. Sweet marjoram *Origanum marjorana*
23. Sage, blue-flowered *Salvia officinalis*
24. Coriander *Coriandrum sativum*
25. Sage, white-flowered *Salvia officinalis albiflora*
26. Honesty, white-flowered *Lunaria annua alba*
27. Giant fennel *Ferula asafoetida*
28. Lady's mantle *Alchemilla vulgaris*
29. Lavender, English *Lavandula vera*
30. French thyme *Thymus vulgare* var. narrow-leaved French
31. Rue *Ruta graveolens*
32. Hyssop, white-flowered *Hyssopus off. albus*
33. Salvia horminum, white-flowered *Salvia horminum* White Bouquet

34. Pot marigold   *Calendula officinalis*
35. True myrtle   *Myrtus communis*
36. Lemon verbena   *Lippia citriodora*
37. Southernwood   *Artemisia abrotanum*
38. Wormwood   *Artemisia absinthium*
39. Woad   *Isatis tinctoria*
40. Sweet fennel   *Foeniculum vulgare*
41. Lovage   *Levisticum officinalis*
42. Foxglove   *Digitalis purpurea*
43. Wood betony   *Stachys betonica*
44. Rosemary   *Rosmarinus officinalis* (white-flowered)
45. Rosemary   *Rosmarinus officinalis* (blue-flowered)
46. Bush Basil   *Ocimum basilicum minimum*
47. Dark opal basil   *Ocimum basilicum* Dark Opal
48. Chives   *Allium schoenoprasum*
49. Summer savory   *Satureja hortensis*
50. Sweet basil   *Ocimum basilicum*
51. Shallots   *Allium ascalonicum*
52. Alpine strawberries   *Fragaria vesca Alexandria*
53. Maryland dittany   *Cunila origanoides*
54. Corsican mint   *Mentha requieni*
55. Pasque flower   *Anemone pulsatilla*
56. English daisies   *Bellis perennis*
57. Winter aconite   *Eranthis hyemalis*
58. White-flowered thrift   *Armeria maritima*
59. Borage   *Borago officinalis*

III

THE EXPANDING HERB GARDEN

In making a garden, there is something to be sought and something to be found. To be sought is a sense of the lovely and assured, of garden permanence and order, of human association and human meaning; to be found is beauty and that unfolding content and occupation which is one of the lamps of peace.

Henry Beston, *Herbs and the Earth*

After all, "The Beginner's Herb Garden" was just a beginning. The following list of additional herbs will bring both beauty and usefulness to your garden.

The culinary herbs for "use"—

Annual	Hardy Perennial	Tender Perennial
Coriander	Burnet	Sweet bay
Dill	Black-stem peppermint	
Shallots	Sweet fennel	
	Lemon balm	
	Lovage	
	Sorrel, French	

For their decorative value, and for "delight"—

Annual	Biennial	Hardy Perennial
Pot marigold	Angelica	Hyssop
	Honesty	Lavender (English)
	Woad	Madonna Lily
		Roof Houseleek
		Rue
		Southernwood

CORIANDER   *Coriander sativum*

This is a charming little annual plant, coming quickly into bloom, from seed sown in early spring, so that a succession of plantings may be made.

The seeds have always been highly esteemed as a condiment, but now the foliage is also being used, in Spain, Mexico, and in California. It is called cilantro, or culantro, or Spanish parsley, depending upon where you are. I have always thought the flavor of the seeds delicious, but have not yet acquired a liking for the leaves.

Coriander is a wild plant in Palestine, and is one of the herbs ordained to be eaten at the time of the Passover. The manna that fell from heaven was compared to coriander seed (Exodus 16:31 and Numbers 11:7). The seed has been found in Egyptian tombs.

DILL   *Anethum graveolens*

Dill is a popular culinary herb today, as in the past, and is a great addition to the herb garden. When it is happy in its location (good soil, full sun) it self-sows so generously that it does not have to be planted again—only transplanted to the location of your choice.

Both leaves and seeds are culinary assets. Even a few plants will produce all the seed you will need. Cut the whole seed head, when it is almost dry, and put it into a paper bag to finish drying. Fresh leaves have many uses, but they lose all flavor in drying. Freeze this herb.

In parts of England, even today, an infusion of dill seeds is given to babies to lull them to sleep. In early America, dill seeds were called meeting seeds, and were nibbled during long church services to keep the congregation awake!

The Romans crowned themselves with garlands of dill, and it was carried by brides in Germany. Dill has always been considered a powerful charm against witchcraft.

Trefoil, vervain, John's wort, dill,
Hinder witches of their will.

This was Gypsy Meg Merrilie's song at the birth of Ham Bertram in Sir Walter Scott's *Guy Mannering*.

SHALLOTS   *Allium ascalonicum*

These are valuable little bulbs, with a mild, onion-like flavor which is yet different from onion. Buy some shallots, and separate the bulbs. Plant them like onions, in early spring, if possible by St. Patrick's Day. Shallots need rich soil, sun and moisture. They are ripe, like onions, when the tops die down, in late August. Dig them up, spread them out on newspapers in a dry place. When they are perfectly dry rub off the soil and loose outside skin of the bulbs, and store them in the refrigerator. They will keep there for a year. Save some of them to plant next season.

BURNET   *Sanguisorba minor*

Often called "salad burnet," this is a pretty perennial plant, decorative in the garden and almost evergreen. It is readily grown from seed, and resents transplanting, but usually comes through. I have sometimes used the leaves in Christmas wreaths. The young leaves are good in a green salad, and taste like cucumber. Many people who do not like cucumber enjoy burnet.

Burnet has been used since ancient times, and has an honorable medical history as a vulnerary, and as a cooling tea in fevers.

BLACKSTEM PEPPERMINT   *Mentha piperita*

This is to me an indispensable herb. It makes my favorite herb tea. All the shady nooks and corners of my garden are planted with it. It has a strong, pungent flavor, and is good hot or iced. It likes a moist, shaded spot. The tea forms the base of a peppermint ice to accompany dinner. For the rare person who does not like spearmint, this herb may be substituted in mint

46

sauce for lamb. Harvest it just as the flowers are beginning to form. Dry; do not freeze.

SWEET FENNEL   Foeniculum officinalis

Sweet fennel is a tall, handsome background plant, with feathered foliage which is useful in flower arrangements. The leaves are used like parsley to flavor fish sauces. In France, fish broiled on a fire of fennel stalks is considered a great delicacy. The seeds are aromatic and are harvested like dill seed. They have been used to flavor confectionery and have culinary possibilities but I have never used them except in salad dressing. The copper-leaved fennel (*consanguineum*) is beautiful but now rare.

This ancient herb was cultivated by the Romans, mentioned by Pliny, Hippocrates and Shakespeare. The juice of the plant was thought to have remarkable powers for restoring eyesight, and the roots, boiled in wine and applied to the eyes, were said to cure cataracts. Those who ate fennel would be brave and strong.

Above the lowly plants it towers
The fennel, with its yellow flowers
And in an earlier age than ours,
Was gifted with the wondrous powers
    Lost vision to restore.

It gave new strength and fearless mood;
And gladiators, fierce and rude,
Mingled it with their daily food;
And he who battled and subdued,
    A wreath of fennel wore.

                    Longfellow, *The Goblet of Life*

LEMON BALM   Melissa officinalis

Lemon balm is a bright green perennial, one of the most

fragrant plants in the garden. It is best used as a tea, and not alone, but in combination with other herbs or with India tea. Start with a plant or two; it can easily be divided at any time after it is established. Dry it; do not freeze.

This is the herb of sympathy, and was used as a strewing herb, and in other ways as a pleasant perfume in the house.

The several chairs of order look you scour
With juice of balm and every precious flower.
Shakespeare, *Merry Wives of Windsor*, act 5, scene 3

Hives were rubbed with balm leaves, because the sweet scent attracted new colonies of bees to the home prepared for them.

Mystic qualities were attributed to balm. Wearing the dried herb in one's clothing made one gay and merry and beloved by everyone.

An old legend concerns the Jew Ahasuerus, who refused a cup of water to the Saviour on his way to Golgotha. The Jew was doomed, therefore, to wander through the world, thirsty, until Christ should come again. On a Whitsuntide evening, Ahasuerus stopped at the door of a cottage in Staffordshire to ask for a drink. It was given to him by a man dying of tuberculosis. Deeply grateful, Ahasuerus told the man to put three balm leaves in his cup of beer, and repeat it every day for twelve days, when the disease would be cured. The Jew departed, never to be seen again, and the cottager was restored to health in twelve days.

LOVAGE   Levisticum officinalis

This tall, hardy perennial plant reaches six or seven feet in height, and was an important ingredient in many old-time recipes. The leaves resemble those of celery, and the flavor is similar but not identical. It is a valuable seasoning for soups, meats and sauces. Lovage is long-lived, because one of my plants is over twenty years old.

Start with a plant. Lovage likes good soil and sunshine, but will happily tolerate some shade.

The leaves dry quickly, and retain a beautiful green color. The seeds are aromatic, and have been used to flavor confectionery. Lovage is enjoying a renewed popularity today, on both sides of the Atlantic.

SORREL, FRENCH   *Rumex scutatus*

Without French sorrel in the herb garden, there would be, alas, no sorrel soup. Begin with plants, and put them in the sun. Sorrel can be used in salads, and is good cooked like spinach, though it is more acid. The arrow-shaped leaves distinguish the culinary French sorrel from the other varieties.

SWEET BAY   *Laurus nobilis*

This tender plant, a tree in its native Mediterranean region, is so delightful to own that it is worth the trouble of finding a greenhouse for a winter retreat. It does not submit to being brought into the house as a potted plant as gracefully as rosemary does, as it seems to need top light.

Getting acquainted with this plant makes one understand what it means to "flourish like the green bay tree." The evergreen leaves are thick, smooth, dark and shining, and they remain that way. Both leaves and stems have a penetrating delightful fragrance. All that a bay tree asks is sun, water and protection from freezing temperatures.

Trips in and out of the greenhouse, and judicious pruning of roots and branches, keep a bay tree a reasonable size. In the spring and again in the fall, offshoots of the roots can be potted as gifts for friends. I dry pruned branches for my supply of bay leaves—a favorite seasoning. They are beautiful even when drying.

My two plants, which stand as sentinels at the entrance to the herb garden, are over twenty years old, and are about four feet tall and two and a half feet in diameter.

This is the laurel that was used to crown poets and warriors in ancient days, when it also had many medicinal uses. I enjoyed making a laurel wreath for a Bethlehem poet several years ago.

Nothing is too much trouble to keep this plant in your collection.

POT MARIGOLD   Calendula officinalis

The pot marigold is a small, single calendula, ancestor of the big, double calendulas that we see in gardens today. It is the only one that belongs in the herb garden. It is ignored by seedsmen in this country, and one has to send to England for seed (Thompson and Morgan, London Road, Ipswich, Suffolk, England). Seed should be sown early; the plants will begin to blossom in July, and continue until hard frost. It does seed itself, but I order fresh seed every year, so as not to lose any of the interesting combinations of color.

The pot marigold has never been a flower to use on the dinner table, since it goes to sleep shamelessly in plain sight of the guests. Recently, however, I have discovered that these flowers, like day lilies with the same early-to-bed motto, can be persuaded to stay open until quite late. Pick them in the morning, and keep them in the refrigerator all day.

For three hundred years, poets and prose writers have been engrossed with the behavior of the pot marigold. They must have been out in their gardens all day long, watching for the flower opening with the dawn, following the sun all day, and closing at sunset. The moisture of the opening blossom did not escape them either, because it was noted that it "rises weeping." More attention was given to the habits of the marigold than to any other flower.

Because their interest has so enchanted me, I may be including too many quotations from these writers. However, I like to look back on an age when men had time to find the movements of a simple little flower so absorbing. I like the quotations, and I like

50

Four Faces
of the
Pot Marigold

the pot marigold, and I hope you will too.

In mediaeval times, these flowers were called "golds," and Chaucer described Jealousy as wearing a garland of them.

In an ancient design depicting jealousy, a marigold flower stands before a shining mirror which is reflecting the rays of the sun, and says, "I die, because he is looking at you."

William Bulleyn, writing in 1562: "The marigold is also named solsequiem because it openeth its flower and turneth around all day after the sun, and closeth in his golden beams at night." From Browne's Pastorals (1613):

But, maiden, see, the day is waxen old
And 'gins to shut in with the marigold.

Thomas Hyll (1577):

This flower is called the husbandsman dyall, for . . . it . . . aptly declareth the hours of the morning and evening by the opening and shutting of it. Also named the sunn's flower, for that after the rising of the sunn until noon, the flower openeth larger and larger, but after the noontime until the setting of the sunn, the flower closeth more and more, and after setting, it is wholly shut up together.

Margaret of Orleans had for her device a marigold turning toward the sun, with the motto "Je ne suivre que lui seul."

John Keats—"I stood tiptoe upon a little hill" (London 1817):

Open fresh your round of starry folds,
Ye ardent marigolds!
Dry up the moisture from your golden lids,
For great Apollo bids
That in these days your praises should be sung
On many harps which he has lately strung;
And when again your dewiness he kisses
Tell him I have you in my world of blisses!

51

So haply when I rove in some far vale
His mighty voice may come upon the gale.

(I love this one of Keats probably most of all.)
Shakespeare made this marigold immortal with his lines about
the "winking Marybuds" in *Cymbeline*:

Hark! Hark! the lark at heaven's gate sings
    And Phoebus 'gins arise,
His steeds to water at those springs
    On chaliced flowers that lies;
And winking Marybuds begin
    To ope their golden eyes;
With everything that pretty is,
    My lady sweet, arise;
    Arise, arise.

And from *The Winter's Tale*:

The marigold that goes to bed with the sun
And with him rises, weeping; these are flowers
Of middle summer, and I think they are given
To men of middle age.   Act 4, scene 3

The monks, in mediaeval England, gave the "gold flower" the
prefix of Mary, with the legend that the Virgin liked to wear
them. Sometimes this came to have a symbolic meaning, as in
Prime's sermon, preached at Oxford on November 17, 1588:
"he . . . professeth that in time to come, he would be no marigold
servant of God, to open with the sun and shut with the dew."
    Instructions for picking this joyous flower are given at length.
It must be taken only when the moon is in the sign of the Virgin,
and not when Jupiter is in the ascendent, for then the herb loses
its virtue. The gatherer must be out of deadly sin, must say three
Pater nosters and three Aves. Among its many virtues, it gives
the wearer a vision of anyone who has robbed him, and just to
look at the flower strengthens the eyes.

Buttercups and marigolds, growing close to each other in Devonshire, are called "publicans and sinners."

The marigold had numerous uses. The yellow and orange petals were formerly used for striking effects in cooking, but opinions about them differed. Parkinson said, "This herb and flower are of great use among the pot herbs, and the flowers are often used in possets and broths and drinks as a comforter of the hearts and spirits." Gerard said, "No broth is well made without dried marigolds." But they did not please Charles Lamb, who, in his essay on "Christ's Hospital" (1823), complained about "boiled beef on Thursday, with detestable marigold petals floating in the pail to poison the broth."

William Turner, the father of English botany, wrote of the marigold (1551): "Some use it to make their hair yellow with the floure of this herb, not being content with the natural color God has given them."

The flowers have long been used as a hemostatic. During the First World War, Miss Gertrude Jekyll gave over a large part of her estate in Sussex for the cultivation of marigold plants. Bushels of petals were shipped from there to the first aid stations in France.

Marigold petals were so used in the American Civil War, as well. Calendula ointment, a soothing dressing for small wounds, is still made.

ANGELICA *Angelica archangelica*

Angelica is a tall, handsome, background plant, with tropical looking foliage and a delightful fragrance. It is happy in a moist spot in partial shade, but the flowers develop better if they are in the sun. It seeds itself, and does not need to be replanted. Only fresh seed are said to be viable, so that it is well to start your angelica by planting fresh seed as soon as it is ripe for blossoming the following year. The plants are said to be perennial if they are not allowed to blossom. Who in the world would want to prevent that? The candied stems of this plant are important in holiday cookery.

The history of angelica is rich in folklore and magic. It was revealed in a dream by an angel, to cure the plague, and it blooms on the day of St. Michael the Archangel. The very name was considered powerful against witchcraft and evil spirits, and it was called "Holy Ghost root." The leaves were tied around the necks of children to protect them from harm. It is said that in East Prussia, peasants chant a song as they carry branches of flowering angelica to market—a song so old, that the words are not understood by the singers themselves, and are probably of pre-Christian origin.

HONESTY *Lunaria annua*

In spite of its botanical name, honesty is a biennial. It is also called moonwort, white satin, satin flower, St. Peter's penny, money flower, penny flower, and money-in-both-pockets.

Plant the seed in good soil in the sun from spring to early summer, for blossoming the following year.

Branches of the seed pods are dried; when completely dry, the outer covering of the pods and the seeds can be easily rubbed off, leaving silvery, moon-like discs which are lovely in winter bouquets.

Honesty is an old herb, which has been affectionately known for centuries, and is grown today in many country gardens in Pennsylvania. The flowers, ranging in color from purple to white, were much used in charms and spells, as was everything else connected with the moon. I think the white-flowering honesty is the most beautiful.

By 1665, it was growing in New England gardens, and was called "honesty" in the writings of the Reverend William Hanbury in 1771.

WOAD *Isatis tinctoria*

Woad is not often seen in herb gardens today, but is really worthy of a place there, as it makes the garden gay in early spring. It grows to four or five feet in height, and is covered with a mist of yellow flowers in May. These are followed by striking black seeds. Woad will grow anywhere, and has been known to seed itself on tennis courts. Once blossoming in the garden, it will never need to be planted again—only transplanted to the places where you want it.

The foliage has a blue-green tinge, which suggests its use. Woad is the blue-dye herb, and has been known for over two thousand years. In 55 B.C. Caesar records that the ancient Britons, before going into battle, painted themselves blue with the juice of this herb, which made them "terrible to see." Woad was grown commercially in England until 1936.

HYSSOP *Hyssopus officinalis*

This hardy perennial plant is an ornament to the herb garden, in specimen plantings or as an attractive low hedge. It reaches a height of fifteen inches when in bloom, but it may be kept clipped to any height desired if one is willing to sacrifice the flowers, which come in pink, blue and white. When buying seed, specify the colors; it is then easy to keep them separated, and have a blue-flowered hedge in one place, and pink and white plantings elsewhere. If wilted flowers are removed, hyssop continues to bloom all summer. The foliage is almost evergreen, except in severe winters, and it can often be cut with other herbs at Christmas.

Hyssop is the sacrificial herb, which was used in cleaning holy places. When Westminster Abbey was consecrated, the altar was sprinkled with hyssop, a continuance of an ancient ceremony.

It is one of the most important bee herbs, today as in ancient times, and gives a fine flavor to honey.

Shakespeare mentions hyssop in *Othello* (Iago's garden sermon.)

MADONNA LILY *Lilum candidum*

The Madonna lily has always belonged in the herb garden, not only because of its ancient medicinal properties, but because of its symbolism. The Benedictine monks had a bed of these lilies at their monastery in St. Gall, Switzerland, in 812.

Both petals and bulb were used for poultices, and the powdered seeds had medicinal uses.

Well known in ancient Greece, it was called "Juno's flower" because it was supposed to have sprung up from the drops of milk which spilled to the ground while Juno was nursing the infant Hercules.

It is probably the white lily of the Bible, and has always been associated with the Virgin. Joseph's staff is said to have blossomed into lilies, and in old paintings of the Annunciation Gabriel always holds a Madonna lily. Because the plant dies down to the ground and disappears, to come up again, fresh and green, the flower also symbolizes the Resurrection.

Plant the bulbs in August in rich, loamy soil with good drainage, which is essential. They will bloom the following June.

LAVENDER *Lavandula officinalis*, English lavender

No herb garden could ever be really complete without lavender, of which there are many lovely species. However, in a cold climate, one must depend upon the truly hardy one, the English lavender, which produces a fine crop of flowers.

These flowers should be harvested at a special time, when the flower at the top of the spike is open, and one or two at the base of the stalk are beginning to fade. Lavender likes sunshine and limestone, and needs careful pruning in the spring, when the plants can easily be divided.

ROOF HOUSELEEK *Sempervivum tectorum*

This ancient herb is one of the familiar hen-and-chickens. Charlemagne commanded his people to plant it on the roofs of their houses, to protect them from lightning, and even today it grows on sod-roofed cottages in Ireland and Wales.

It forms an endearing little rosette, and does indeed live

forever—or until it blooms, when it sends up one great flower stalk and dies (but always leaves many descendants). Up to that time, it will stand anything; dogs and squirrels can dig it up and toss it around, and days later it can be replanted and survive. It makes a lovely edging for a bed of herbs. Buy a few plants, and separate them as the chickens multiply.

RUE   *Ruta graveolens*

Rue is a lovely perennial plant, with lacy, blue-green foliage and charming yellow flowers, which remains beautiful far into the fall. It has a bitter fragrance which is quite different from any other. It comes easily from seed, but I would start with plants. Rue likes a friable, alkaline soil in a sunny situation. It should be cut back in the fall. When the last chrysanthemums have gone, I bring bowls of rue into the house and they console me for two weeks.

Rue is sometimes identified as the moly which Mercury gave to Ulysses to help him withstand the enchantments of Circe. An old superstition persists that rue thrives better if stolen from a friend's garden.

Two years ago I saw an enormous plant of rue—the largest I had ever seen. It belonged to Mrs. Matthews, a member of the congregation of the Moravian Morongo Mission to the Indians, in Banning, California. When I admired the plant, calling it by name, Mrs. Matthews said they did not know it as rue, but called it the Mexican plant, because a Mexican had given it to them. She reported that it was an infallible cure for earache. Roll up a few leaves, tuck them in your ear, and the relief is immediate.

Rue is the herb of grace, of repentance, understanding, contrition. In *Hamlet*, Ophelia offered it to the Queen to wear.

SOUTHERNWOOD   *Artemisia abrotanum*

This is a long lived perennial plant with finely cut gray foliage and a pungent fragrance. It will succeed in ordinary garden soil in the sun, will even tolerate a little shade. It is really a small shrub, which tends to become woody unless carefully pruned. Start with a plant.

This is the herb of constancy. It was called "lad's love" because young boys believed that rubbing the ashes of this plant on their faces would hasten the growing of a beard. The name "old man" was used, because the fine, gray foliage suggests age.

Southernwood had potency as a love charm, and cured sleepwalking. The Pennsylvania Germans spread branches of southernwood around the house to keep out ants, and in France it is strewn on the floor of clothes closets as a moth preventive.

Lenten Rose

Pasque Flower

Crown Imperial

Saffron Crocus

Christmas Rose

Five Very Special Herbs

IV

FIVE VERY SPECIAL HERBS THAT
BLOOM VERY EARLY AND VERY LATE

LENTEN ROSE   Helleborus orientalis

This close relative of the Christmas Rose is a great delight in the spring. I have one plant, twelve years old, which produces about seventy-five dark red blossoms during Lent. It seems to know just when Easter is coming, and the blossoming varies a little according to the date. It is a charming cut flower, and if it is stored in the refrigerator between dinners, it will decorate the dining table for a week. My plant is growing under a dogwood tree, and seems to like that situation, where it gets no summer sun.

PASQUE FLOWER   Anemone pulsatilla

The beauty of the Pasque flower, which blooms in late March, heralding Easter, would seem enough reason for its existence. In addition, it has been important in medicine. A few drops of tincture of pulsatilla allays the cough of asthma, whooping cough and bronchitis; it has been valuable in eye infections and in treating cataracts and relieves headaches, neuralgia and nerve exhaustion.

THE CROWN IMPERIAL   Fritilleria imperialis

This stately lily, symbolizing majesty and power, is a native of Persia, Afghanistan and Kashmir. It was taken to Constantinople, and then to Vienna in 1576, and finally to England during the Renaissance. In China, the crown imperial was considered to be a valuable tonic for the bone marrow, for fevers and for eye disorders. It seems rather horrible to record that in Persia the bulbs, each holding a magnificent flower, were cooked and eaten. Fresh, the bulbs are poisonous.

An unpleasant scent, which is always compared to that of a fox or skunk, emanates from the roots, and seems to warn young animals not to eat it. A calf will not approach it from a distance of five yards.

In "La Botanique," Stephanie de St. Aubin described a magnificent album which the Duc de Montansier presented to his bride, Julie de Rambouillet, on New Year's Day, 1643. Each page of this celebrated book, which was called *La Guirlande de Julie*, bore a beautifully painted flower and a madrigal describing it. On one page appears a painting of the crown imperial. Chapelain chose it for his theme, pretending that it sprang from the blood of Sweden's Gustavus Adolphus, who, not being able to offer his hand to Julie, came to her in the guise of this flower.

Stephanie, writing in 1811, reports that *La Guirlande de Julie* was sold in Hamburg in 1795, and that the name of the purchaser was not known.

Because of my long enchantment with this flower, I wanted to see this album. This was not one book of a printing; this was the only *Guirlande de Julie* in all the world.

Where was it now? Anything so beautiful should not be lost. I wrote to the Morgan Library in New York, asking whether they knew where I could see it. By return mail I received a copy of their library card for *La Guirlande de Julie*. Another treasure had found sanctuary in that wonderful library forever.

John Parkinson says: "The Crown Imperial, for his stately beautifulness, deserveth the first place in this our Garden of Delight, to be here entreated of before all other lilies."

There is a legend that the crown imperial grew in the Garden of Gethsemane, and that on the night of Christ's agony, it was the only flower that did not bow its head in grief. Later, this proud flower, full of remorse, bent its head, and tears of sorrow filled its cup. Its head will remain bowed, and its tears will continue to flow, forever.

Melanie and Crown Imperials

If the tears are removed, new ones form. Parkinson says: "Inside [the flower] there lieth certain clear drops of water, like unto pearls, of a very sweet taste, almost like sugar."

The "pearls and tears" are beautiful, and well worth the effort it takes to see them.

SAFFRON CROCUS *Crocus sativus*

Late in October, when the herbs are settling down quietly for the winter, there will come a morning when suddenly the herb garden is a blaze of color. Somehow it is always a surprise to me to find the saffron crocuses in bloom.

Even if, like me, you find little culinary merit in the flavor of saffron used alone, you will find that the blooming of this ancient herb is an annual delight. Give bulbs for August planting to friends with October birthdays.

Saffron is a legacy to us from the ancients, a plant with a history of use as a medicine, a dye, and a perfume. It traveled early to Egypt, where it was grown and used for thousands of years. When Sir Aurel Stein was digging along some of the trade routes in the Egyptian desert, he uncovered a roll of silk dyed with the sacred imperial yellow of saffron. Lost from some caravan, it had been covered with sand for two thousand years, and the color was perfectly preserved.

Saffron was included in Hippocrates' list of four hundred medicinal herbs, and it grew in Solomon's garden.

The three brilliant red-orange stigmas of the flower are the parts used, and as one ounce of saffron represents the product of four thousand flowers, it has always commanded a high price. It is fun and easy to harvest one's own saffron. Young virgins wore saffron-colored robes to denote chastity, and in 534 B.C. Aeschylus wrote that when Iphigenia was sacrificed at the altar by her father, she was wearing a saffron robe.

CHRISTMAS ROSE *Helleborus niger*

The season which commenced with the blooming of the

61

Lenten rose, last spring, comes to a lovely end with the blossoming of the Christmas rose in November and December.

Grown in the auspicious setting of "winter sun and summer shade," the great *Helleborus niger* will go on blooming for many years. Often surrounded by ice and snow, this incredible plant blossoms in November and December.

I have been told that in Germany, in old houses with stone walls three feet thick, Christmas roses are grown in pots between the inside window and the storm sash, where they blossom profusely.

Culpeper attributed many virtues to this poisonous plant; the roots were effective in "quartan agues and madness"; they helped leprosy and the "falling sickness." Pliny says that the roots were used as a purgative in mania 1400 years before Christ. Applied locally, the fresh root is a violent irritant, but Hippocrates used it in an ointment.

A native plant of Mt. Athos, and of the hills of Thessalonia, where Tournefort found it, it has been cultivated in England since 1596.

HERB GARDEN
ON THE GREEN

CENTRAL MORAVIAN CHURCH
BETHLEHEM, PENNSYLVANIA

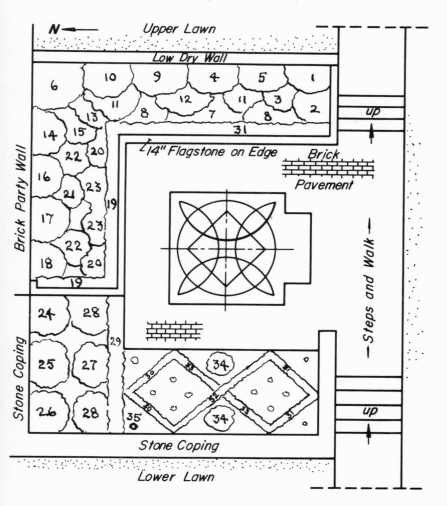

Each of the twelve small circles in the west bed denotes the location of one saffron crocus bulb, although only one of them is marked with the key number 35. These bulbs may seem to destroy the design of the garden, but actually they do not. The saffron crocus appears briefly in the spring, showing a few grasslike leaves. These disappear almost at once, and there is no further sign of life in the bulb until just before the late October blooming.

The knot in the center bed is planted in English boxwood.

KEY TO PLANTING
IN THE HERB GARDEN ON THE GREEN

1. Sweet cicely — *Myrrhis odorata*
2. Sweet woodruff — *Asperula odorata*
3. Lungwort — *Pulmonaria officinalis*
4. Loosestrife — *Lysimachia punctata*
5. Costmary — *Chrysanthemum balsamita*
6. Bergamot — *Monarda didyma*
7. Lambs' Ears — *Stachys lanata*
8. Pot marigold — *Calendula officinalis*
9. Rosemary — *Rosmarinus officinalis*
10. White sage, western mugwort — *Artemisia ludoviciana*
11. Dark Opal basil — *Ocimum basilicum Dark Opal*
12. Hyssop, white flowered — *Hyssopus officinalis*
13. Lavender cotton — *Santolina chamaecyparissus*
14. Madonna lilies — *Lilium candidum*
15. Herb Bennett, Benoit — *Geum coccineus*
16. Korean mint — *Agastache rugosa*
17. Agrimony — *Agrimonia eupatoria*
18. Wormwood — *Artemisia absinthium*
19. Trailing wooly thyme — *Thymus lanicaulis*
20. Sage — *Salvia officinalis*
21. Horehound — *Marrubium vulgare*
22. Feverfew — *Matricaria parthenium*
23. French thyme — *Thymus vulgare* var. narrow-leaved French
24. Elecampane — *Inula helenium*
25. Angelica — *Angelica archangelica*
26. Lovage — *Levisticum officinale*
27. Pasque flower — *Anemone pulsatilla*
28. Rue — *Ruta graveolens*
29. Catmint — *Nepeta mussini*
30. Thrift, white-flowered — *Armeria maritima alba*

31.	Thrift, pink-flowered	*Armeria maritima rubra*
32.	Germander	*Teucrium chamaedrys*
33.	Hyssop	*Hyssopus officinalis*
34.	Alpine strawberry	*Fragaria vesca Alexandria*
35.	Saffron crocus	*Crocus sativus*

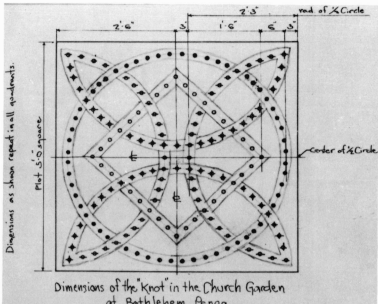

Dimensions of the "Knot" in the Church Garden
at Bethlehem, Penna.

After a Sketch in "The Gardener's Labyrinth"
by Dydymus Mountaine (Thomas Hyll), 1577.

To adapt to a plot of a different size, alter all
dimensions in proportion to length of plot side.

Number of Plants as shown:
● 56. ○ 32. ◉ 46. ◆ 46. Total - 180.

(For the Church Garden at Bethlehem,
box was used throughout for simplicity).

f 1957
D.

THE KNOT GARDEN

Bethlehem attracts many visitors in the course of a year—visitors from all over the world. They come to see the fine old stone houses which were built in the early days of the settlement. They come at Christmas, to see the Community Putz, and to see the lighted city, with a candle burning in almost every window.

Guides in gray and white early Moravian costumes take guests first to see Central Church, which, built in 1806, is the newest of the buildings in the Moravian group. Then they go to the Gemein Haus (congregation house), which was the first place of worship in the town, and to the Old Chapel, which was the second. The Gemein Haus, on which construction commenced in 1742, is the oldest building. The Sisters' House and the Widows' House have been residences all these years, and the latter is still being used for its original purpose.

Visitors are nothing new in Bethlehem. From 1741 until the present day there has always been something of interest here to see or to study. George Washington came, and Benjamin Franklin, and the Marquis de la Fayette, who recuperated here from the wounds he received in the Battle of the Brandywine. Every member of the Continental Congress passed through the Gemein Haus door. The story of Bethlehem's visitors, through the years, is a long and fascinating tale.

Today's visitors are taken to see the Old Apothecary Shop, and sooner or later, many of them visit the herb garden on the Green. Through the years, various plantings have succeeded each other in this garden, but the one which almost everyone has liked best is the boxwood knot in the center bed, which was planted in 1957.

For two or three years before that, in my garden at home, I had been experimenting with knots using interlacing gray and green herbs. I could not report much success. To keep the pattern true required a great deal of time, and I was not satisfied with even my best efforts.

John Parkinson described his experience with knots in 1629. I found that my germander, like his, would "grow out of form," and that "the roots would spread to many places within the knot." My lavender cotton, like his, could, by cutting, "be kept in even proportions," but in spite of that, would soon "grow too great."

He had other complaints, which he summed up by saying that

All these herbs will force you to take up your knot sooner than if it were planted in box, which lastly, above all other herbs, I recommend to you, to set out any knot . . . for besides that it is evergreen, it . . . will be easily cut and formed into any fashion one will. The nature thereof is to grow slowly, and will not, in a long time, rise to any height. This I commend and hold to be the surest herb to abide fair and green in all the bitter storms of sharpest winter and all the great heat and droughts of summer.

My own experience has proved that Parkinson's advice is as timely today as it was in the seventeenth century. However, he suggested dwarf Dutch box, and this garden was planted in three-inch rooted cuttings of English box.

I am including the plan for this very simple design from which we worked in planting the church garden. Any interested reader can readily duplicate it. Who knows? Perhaps, to some one, Parkinson's words will be a challenge to inspire the planting of this knot garden in four contrasting herbs. This would be easy to do, by using the symbols in the design.

No planting could be simpler to care for than a boxwood knot. In the spring, the thick mulch of peat moss is removed, the plants trimmed into shape, the ground cultivated and fertilized, and a little ground limestone sprinkled on top of the soil around the plants. Box accepts either acid or alkaline soil, but I have always used limestone. The mulch is then replaced, and more added if necessary. The knot will need observation, but no real attention for about two months. Now and then a plant has to be replaced, usually because of dog-damage, but not often. The knot is always watered well in dry spells.

One thing that I know is important to the success of the planting is the really great cover that goes over it in winter. The sides are wood, about a foot high, and the top is wire screening, reinforced with strips of wood. This cover lets in light and air, but protects the boxwood from snow. Snow lying on the foliage for any length of time could be fatal. The cover is put on sometime in October, and removed during March, or early April, the exact dates depending upon the weather.

V

HARVESTING THE HERBS

Flavor and fragrance in the herbs are said to reach their peak just as their flowers are beginning to open. This is the best time for harvesting the crop. Choose a hot summer morning, after the dew has disappeared, and the leaves are dry. Even if you have plenty of time, it is better to pick only two or three crops in one day. It always takes longer than you expect to care for them.

When the fresh crop is brought in, drop it into deep cold water, wash it gently, and drain it in colanders for at least a half hour. Inspect it carefully for wilted and imperfect leaves and treat it just as carefully as though it were lettuce for a salad.

Long before I ever harvested an herb, I heard my aunt tell a story about a father who was visiting his newly married daughter for the first time. She had taken him on a tour of her new home, and when it was over, the father looked puzzled. "Where is your attic?" he asked. The daughter replied, "We have no attic, Father." The father said, "Heaven help you, Daughter, if you haven't an attic!"

Aunty had had an attic all her life, and so have I, so the drying of herbs has never been a problem. All that is necessary is there—heat, ventilation, and air circulating through the foliage.

At present I dry my herbs on a drying stand with four shelves of screening each measuring fifteen by twenty inches. Before I had this, I used to spread out the herbs on old sheets on the attic floor. When the whole plant is pulled up at harvest time (for example, sweet basil and summer savory), the plants can be hung by the roots from the rafters. Smaller clippings can be dried in paper bags left open at the top.

Lacking an attic, find the driest, warmest place in the house. I found a great little drying spot in my kitchen at one time, when I discovered that the six-inch space between the top of the refrigerator and the cupboard above it was so well heated by the motor of the refrigerator that a small crop of herbs would be dry to brittle crispness in two days. This was useful for drying the leaves from one bunch of celery.

Regardless of the method you use, be sure to label each crop, with the date of harvest. This is important because the herbs look quite different when dry. In hot weather, drying takes only a few days. Then put each crop, with its dated label, into its own paper bag, to await the time when it is convenient to transfer each one to a permanent air-tight container. This then makes room on the drying stand for subsequent crops.

FREEZING THE HERBS

Freezer space is at a much higher premium in my house than shelf space, so, unless a frozen herb tastes much better than its dried counterpart, I do not freeze it.

There are three herbs which I always freeze but never dry. They are chives, chervil and parsley—the classic *fines herbes*. Not one of them has much flavor dry, though they can be so used if there are no freezing facilities available. Chervil, especially, dries a lovely green so that it is pretty, even if it tastes only faintly of chervil.

Even though I like my dried tarragon very much—it is pungent, and full of flavor—I still like to freeze part of the crop for salads and for special chicken dishes, keeping the leaves whole.

I like rosemary better fresh, but I can pick that from my plants all winter.

All the other herbs are used dried, in my house, and I am pleased with them that way. Some taste much better dried, such as sage and sweet woodruff. The latter develops its maximum flavor only in drying.

THE DRIED HERBS

Presently the time comes to remove the dried herbs from their paper bags and store them permanently in airtight jars. Try to keep the leaves of the tea herbs as nearly whole as possible when you remove them from the stems. All the other herbs, after the leaves are picked off the stems, may be put through a coarse sieve. Label the containers in India ink with the name of the herb and the date of harvest. At the end of a year, when the new crop comes in, discard any that are left—all except the mints, which seem to keep their flavor and fragrance almost indefinitely.

In colonial days, "papering the herbs" was a pleasant occupation for a long winter evening. It is still one of the most agreeable ways to spend a few hours. Friends enjoy being invited to help, and the house will be full of delightful odors for a week.

Some of the most beautifully dried herbs I have seen were dried by artificial heat. I remember a visit to the charming kitchen-dining room of Crosby Gaige, many years ago. This room was adjacent to the herb garden, and in it was a small oven designed just for drying herbs. I can still see the beautiful green of the parsley that came out of that oven.

The drying rooms on the herb farm of Marc Darbonne at Milly-la-Forêt, in France, are never-to-be-forgotten. Approaching this town on the bus from Paris, you pass winding creeks, crystal clear, full of lush, green watercress. That watercress, dried in specially designed ovens, came out looking even more green than it was in the creek.

Drying herbs in a home oven is a different matter. I believe it can be done, but it requires special knowledge of the exact temperatures needed for each herb, and constant watching. Even then, catastrophe is always imminent. It is ever so much easier to take the crops to the attic and forget them.

VI

MAKING HERB-FLAVORED VINEGARS

When there are herb vinegars at hand in the kitchen, new uses are found for them continually. Sometimes a tablespoon of a flavored vinegar will perform a kind of magic. It does something special, for instance, for a pot of vegetable soup which for some reason, in spite of your best efforts, tastes a little flat. You may want just a touch of garlic in something, and a half teaspoon of garlic-flavored vinegar will do wonders. Even fruit cups are not immune to a little help from a flavored vinegar.

The flavors that I find most useful are tarragon, spearmint, garlic, burnet, a combination of burnet and shallot, and sweet basil.

The possibilities for experimentation are endless, using citrus rinds, spices and rose geranium leaves.

TARRAGON:

Fill a quart jar with tarragon leaves, which have been carefully washed, inspected, and drained. Add five cracked peppercorns. Fill the jar with cider vinegar and cover it with a non-corrosive lid. Let it stand for several weeks, at least three, rolling the contents around occasionally. Then strain the vinegar to remove the leaves, and afterward put it through a filter. A wet coffee filter paper in a strainer will do very well. Pour the vinegar into glass bottles, and add a sprig of the fresh herb for identification. Laboratory bottles of the kind used for acids are attractive and inexpensive, and the tinted liquids look pretty in these clear glass containers.

SPEARMINT:

Follow the directions for tarragon vinegar, substituting spearmint leaves for tarragon, and omitting peppercorns. Use either cider or white wine vinegar. Complete as directed, using a blossoming tip of spearmint in each bottle.

GARLIC:

Separate the cloves of a big bulb of garlic. Peel and halve them, and put them into a quart jar. Fill the jar with either cider or red wine vinegar, and cover it with a non-corrosive lid. Let stand at least three weeks, rolling the contents around once in a while. Strain, filter and bottle like tarragon vinegar, and add a peeled clove of garlic in each bottle.

BURNET:

Follow the directions for tarragon vinegar, substituting burnet leaves for tarragon and omitting peppercorns. Finish by putting a whole burnet leaf in each bottle.

BURNET AND SHALLOT:

Follow directions for burnet vinegar, adding five good-sized peeled and halved shallots. Complete as directed, using a whole burnet leaf and one shallot in each bottle.

SWEET BASIL:

Follow directions for burnet vinegar, substituting basil leaves for burnet leaves. Complete as directed, using a blossoming tip of sweet basil.

AFTERTHOUGHTS

We have planted a Beginner's Herb Garden, and we have expanded that garden, and I am dismayed at the number of lovely plants that have been left out. A few of them must be mentioned by name.

The true myrtle (*Myrtis communis*) is a tender perennial shrub, whose leaves crowned the warriors and poets of old. Today they are worn by modern brides in Norway and in Germany. It is a lovely plant to own, because of the gentle fragrance of its leaves, and for its exquisite white blossoms. It must go into a pot in a greenhouse in winter, in cold climates.

The star jasmine (*Jasminum officinalis*) is a pretty vining plant with white star-like flowers so fragrant that just one of them, opening in a small greenhouse, will fill it with perfume. In southern France, near Grasse, this jasmine is grown in large fields, and the flowers are harvested singly, by hand, for the perfume factories. The perfume from these great baskets of flowers reaches the motorists on the nearby roads.

Lady's mantle (*Alchemilla vulgaris*), a hardy perennial of cold climates, brings design into the herb garden. Its neatly pleated, pointed leaves resemble a lady's cloak. It brings something else, which resembles a king's ransom in diamonds. Every morning the margins of these leaves are outlined in dew drops which sparkle as no other dew drops anywhere ever sparkled.

The smallest herb of all, the creeping Corsican mint (*Mentha requieni*) has tiny leaves which hold the strongest of all peppermint fragrances. It is not supposed to be hardy in my garden, but it is.

Maryland dittany (*Cunila origanoides*) is a charming little American herb, a hardy perennial. It is used today on its native heath as a tea to relieve a headache. It is pretty in fresh or in dried bouquets.

Coltsfoot (*Tussilago farfara*) always surprises me in the spring, when its lovely single flower appears, flat on the ground, with no leaf in sight anywhere. "Son before the father." Last spring I saw a hillside of it in bloom along the Pennsylvania turnpike, and wondered by what route that European herb had arrived at its destination. The "son" is much more entrancing than the "father." Coltsfoot salve, a healing preparation, is still available in old-fashioned drug stores today.

All the thymes deserve close acquaintance, and the great dittany of Crete (*Amaracus dictamnus*), a potted plant all the year, has a long story all its own.

Try to become acquainted with them all some day.

VII

LITTLE HERBAL DELIGHTS

Having a collection of herbs at hand leads to all sorts of pleasant uses, which seem to bring enjoyment to family and friends. I always hope there is as much joy in receiving as there is in the giving.

Blossoming tips of the herbs are charming in small nosegays, like the tussie-mussies of the seventeenth century. These little bouquets, made up of whatever herbs are prettiest at the moment, make much-appreciated little gifts in many situations. The tiniest go nicely into letters; one of these, or a sprig of rosemary, or the big flat, fragrant leaf of a scented geranium makes a letter come to life.

In writing to a little granddaughter, I always enclose something green and fragrant. One day she wrote me the following: "I love the things you put in my letters. I have a friend who never gets ANYTHING in a letter. This is her address. Will you please write a letter to her and put some rosemary in it?" It was done, and a letter came back from Dorrie's friend right away.

Especially lovely in these nosegays are miniature rosebuds, and, if the bouquet is to go into a vase, the flowers and fruit of the Alpine strawberry. If attractive containers are kept on hand, it is always easy to put together some herbs and roses for a hospital patient. These simple offerings have often proved to be more popular with friends, ill or well, than a handsome gift from the florist.

This is hard to understand unless one realizes that the very word *herb* carries a kind of magic today—as perhaps it always has, in the past. An ill person finds pleasure in the fragrance of a sprig of rosemary, or lavender, or thyme, held in the hand, and a convalescent likes to try to identify the herbs in a bouquet. To the blind, these herbs are eloquent indeed.

With a bowl of blooming herbs, a pair of sharp scissors and a jar of rubber cement, it is fun to make herbal birthday cards using plain greeting cards which are available in stores carrying artists' supplies. Herbal place cards are pretty and interesting, and little bouquets decorate gift packages all the year. At Christmas, it is a sprig of rosemary or bay.

At Christmas, make a big fragrant wreath for the front door, using the evergreen herbs, rosemary, bay, lavender, thyme, sage and myrtle. Small wreaths decorate less important doors. Frames made of chicken wire can be used year after year.

In the Christmas "Putz," the nativity scene which is so important a part of the Moravian Christmas, the bed of the Christ Child is lined with the traditional herbs, thyme, bedstraw, and pennyroyal, which is supposed to bloom at midnight!

All through the year, there should be a piece of rosemary in the bridal bouquet of any friend who is being married. Every one of my "Rosemary Brides" has remained happily wedded!

Herbs which are destined to be used in any of the ways suggested should be picked far ahead, so that they can be kept in water in a cold place for several hours, or overnight. Hardened in this way, just like any flowers to be used in an arrangement, they keep beautifully, retaining form and color. Birthday cards are often kept from year to year, and sometimes framed, like flower pictures.

Who can say that these simple things have no importance?

A Birthday Card from the Herb Garden

VIII

COOKING WITH HERBS

Better is a dinner of herbs, where love is, than a stalled ox and hatred therewith.   Proverbs 15:17

At its best, food well-cooked is simple, and depends for success upon countless small perfections, such as attractive combinations of color, pleasing contrasts in texture, and well-blended flavor. There is art in the contrast of creamy filling and crisp crust; in the shad which slides out of the oven on its plank, perfectly done, but dripping with moisture; in the baked custard which is soft, yet holds its shape, without a single bubble to reproach the cook with oven too hot, or cooking time too long; in a salad in which every leaf glistens with oil, yet there is not a drop in the bottom of the bowl; in a meringue with a sparkling crust, crisp on top, creamy underneath, but never sticking to your fork, and the whole perfectly flavored.

Flavor is an important part of the magic of good cooking; it may be the touch of lemon juice in the chicken livers, the combination of shallots and sour cream in the scrambled eggs, the addition of a little sugar to many foods—to the pot of vegetable soup, to anything containing tomatoes, to the white onions when they are ready for the cream sauce. There are all sorts of seasoning helps right at our fingertips, such as the richly-flavored rinds of oranges, lemons and limes, which do wonderful things to make food surprising and delicious.

The herbs are important additions to this list. They often make simple foods taste better. While I admire the *haute cuisine*, and like to try my hand at something in that category occasionally, I have always been more interested in the simple *pot au feu* that the great chef has for dinner when he goes home at night, than I am in the elaborate concoctions he puts together during the day.

If it is important to learn to use the herbs to achieve good flavor, it is just as important to learn when not to use them. Long printed lists of herbs to use with fish, herbs to use with eggs, herbs to put in the salad are helpful in the very beginning of one's culinary adventures with the herbs, but soon, with certain limitations, your use of herbs becomes just a matter of personal preferences.

The flavor of rosemary I find delicious, yet I would never touch a sprig of rosemary to a prime rib roast of beef, though I often read recipes advising it. Nor would I add an herb, any herb, to mushrooms served alone. Butter, salt, and perhaps cream, are all they need. Strongly flavored foods like Boston mackerel or smoked ham need no herbs; they have enough flavor already. Some delicately flavored foods, like crabmeat, might have their own flavor changed by the addition of an herb. Lemon juice, yes. Few vegetables need herbs if served fresh from the garden. Carrots, however, are delicious cooked with tarragon, once in a while; creamed celery is improved by the addition of celery seed, and most squashes gain by extra seasoning.

An herb, or any combination of herbs, should enhance a flavor without altering it, and should make the food taste good without dominating it. So, until your own preferences and those of your family develop, it is safer to use a very light touch with the herbs. After a while you will find that there are places where a light touch is not enough, and you may develop a heavy hand with certain herbs in certain dishes. I know that I have a heavy hand with curry, and also with sage when it goes into sausage, scrapple and poultry stuffing.

CULINARY SUGGESTIONS

Remember that one teaspoon of the more concentrated dried herb is equivalent to two teaspoons of the fresh or frozen.

Crumble the dried herb to a powder in your hand before using it; cut the frozen leaves with sharp scissors; put the fresh herb through the *mouli persil*, that invaluable French "parsley mill" which is available almost everywhere.

For seasoning meat, the following have been found good: sage, sweet marjoram, dill, summer savory, basil, rosemary and thyme. For cheese and egg dishes, there are chervil, chives and tarragon. For salads there are tarragon, burnet, chervil and chives; and for fish, fennel, basil and bay. Basil has always been called the "tomato herb," and summer savory has been named the "bean herb," the German *bohnenkraut*.

However, it will soon be discovered that the meat herb, sage, gives a delicious flavor to a special loaf of bread. The salad herb tarragon is a wonderful addition to chicken. A bay leaf is so versatile it adds delicious flavor not only to meat and fish but also to a holiday cake. The uses of rosemary are almost unlimited.

Sesame seed is indispensable, and almost universally liked. Sesame was an ancient herb, growing in the Nile Valley when Pharaoh's daughter found Moses in the bulrushes. It was brought to America from Africa by Negro slaves. To them it was a symbol of good luck, and was so important in their lives and their food that their masters continued to import it for them. They called it "benne," meaning health, and indeed the seed is rich in protein, oil and minerals. The benne seed cookies of Charleston are famous. It has so many uses that I buy it by the pound, and think of Ali Baba when I use it.

The candied stems of angelica are a delightful adjunct to holiday cookery. They form the tiny stems and leaves of the flowers that decorate *petits-fours* and *biscuit tortoni*, and are good in other fancy frozen desserts. They not only look pretty but taste good, reminding one of the wonderful, absolutely unique fragrance of the whole angelica plant.

Efforts are made to candy these stems in this country, but without much success. Since they do them superbly in France, I am content to let them do some for me, while my own angelica plants rise to their full six feet of glory.

HERBAL TEAS

Then there are the herb teas, which are called *tisanes* in France, where the word has a somewhat medical connotation. Even so, they are more generally used there than in our country, and are always obtainable in restaurants even when they do not appear on the menu.

A great interest in the *tisanes* is developing here, as part of the excited concern about herbs in general. Perhaps the knowledge that these teas are good for you has something to do with it.

A liking for them is not really an acquired taste, for if you accept in the beginning the fact that none of them is going to taste like orange pekoe or Formosa oolong, you will like them at once. You will have your favorites, of course, but served plain, or with lemon and honey, they are truly delicious.

Many of them you can easily grow in quantity, given the necessary space. My favorite is English black-stem peppermint. Others I depend upon are sweet woodruff, bergamot, spearmint, lemon balm, lemon verbena and Korean mint (*Agastache rugosa*). It is worth noting that the latter is a comparative newcomer in this country, in contrast to all the other herbs mentioned. Korean mint was first introduced to America by an army officer who brought it back from the Korean War. It is a popular tea in Korea and a wonderful bee plant anywhere. Like its close relative, *Agastache foeniculum*, the bees hang upon the flowers until long after dark. Both plants have a penetrating fragrance and a fine flavor.

These teas can be made up in mixtures of your own selection or used alone. I always use the black peppermint alone, but spearmint may be mixed with an equal amount of a favorite black tea, with excellent results. Lemon balm and lemon verbena are better in combination.

Chamomile, Peter Rabbit's tea, linden (the French *tilleul*, a mixture of the leaves and flowers of the linden tree), fenugreek and vervain can all be bought, and there are excellent herbal mixtures available from the good commercial herb growers.

If you doubt the current interest in these beverages, make an experiment the next time you have some people in for tea. Put a pot of Earl Grey or some other favorite tea at one end of the table, and a good herb tea at the other end. Then observe which teapot has to be refilled first.

A *tisane* is good at almost any time, late at night, if coffee keeps you awake, or even if it doesn't. If you are especially tired or if you have the beginning of a cold or if you are perfectly well and just want a cup of tea, enjoy one with many extra benefits. For most of us, this is a wonderful new field to explore.

Herb teas have other uses, too. Peppermint or spearmint tea makes the base of a delicious ice, to accompany dinner. This can be kept on hand in the freezer.

A QUICK TOUCH OF HERBS

The flavor of a single herb is good in cream cheese which has been softened with a little cream. Add salt, and a bit of sugar if you like; try sweet marjoram, or thyme, sweet basil, or spearmint, or dill. Use this as a filling for small, open tea sandwiches, and garnish with the fresh herb when possible.

Use these cream cheese mixtures to make balls, the size of a pie cherry, and mix them with the greens in a salad bowl.

Chopped spearmint, mixed with sugar, makes an interesting little tea sandwich.

To canned tomato soup, add a pinch of sweet or opal basil, while it is heating.

Try seasoning bean soup, home made or canned, with sage, sweet marjoram, summer savory and thyme.

Add rosemary and summer savory to baked beans, home made or canned.

Make a little bunch of fresh herbs, a bay leaf, a few sprigs of parsley, some thyme and some celery leaves. Tie it together with a white thread and drop it into soup or stew an hour before it has finished cooking. This is the French *bouquet garni.* It is, of course, removed before serving.

When cooking carrots, try adding to them a few minced shallots and some diced celery. Use only a small amount of boiling water and simmer until the carrots are done and the water has evaporated. Season with butter, salt, sugar and minced parsley.

When making hamburgers for freezing, try mixing one teaspoon of dried thyme with one pound of ground beef. Form into patties, and wrap each separately. Store them in a large container in the freezer, so that it will be easy to take out just the number needed.

For breakfast, try sprinkling a few minute snippings of fresh rosemary on a half grapefruit which has been sweetened with honey.

For luncheon, all the herb soups are good—watercress, sorrel, and leek-and-potato. Leek-and-potato hot becomes *vichysoisse* when cold, with a change of garnishes (grated raw carrot and parsley for the hot, finely cut chives for the cold).

For dinner, try serving a good consomme, in which a few finely diced vegetables have been briefly cooked—carrot, celery, onion. Garnish it with one-quarter teaspoon fresh or frozen minced tarragon to each cup.

Cooking? Cooking with herbs? All good cooking turns out to be cooking with love.

RECIPES

Please read these notes before using these recipes, so that instructions will not have to be repeated each time.

All measurements are level.

All oven and frying pan temperatures are preheated.

It is assumed that all herbs, except bay leaves, bouquets garnis, and tea herbs, will be made fine before incorporating with food. Dry herbs should be crumbled to a powder; fresh herbs should be minced in the *mouli persil* (parsley mill) or cut fine with sharp scissors, or chopped fine on a board. Chives must always be cut very fine with scissors.

Sifted before measuring—s.b.m.

One cup = 1 c.
One teaspoon = 1 t.
One tablespoon = 1 T.

Whenever pepper is mentioned, it means freshly ground black pepper.

All herbs used in these recipes, except three, are dried herbs, unless "fresh" is specified.

Chives, chervil and parsley will always be fresh or frozen. 1 t. of a fresh herb = 1 t. of a frozen herb.

When substituting a fresh for a dried herb, remember that 1 t. fresh herb = 1/2 t. dried herb.

APPETIZERS

CURRY-CHIVES DIP

1 3 oz. pkg. cream cheese (room temperature)
1/2 c. sour cream
1/4 t. salt
1 T. plus 1 t. Daw Sen curry powder
3 T. finely cut chives

Mix first three ingredients, ending by beating with a wire whisk. Blend in curry powder and chives. Store in a covered jar in refrigerator, and allow to ripen several hours. Serve with tiny crackers the size of a dime. With another appetizer or two, this will serve eight. Cubes of Caerphilly cheese on toothpicks and whole pecans go well with it.

CHICKEN LIVER PATÉ

4 slices paper thin lean bacon
1 T. butter
1 lb. chicken livers
1 T. onion juice
1 t. salt
1/4 t. nutmeg, grated
2 grindings black pepper
1 T. fresh lemon juice
3 T. dry sherry
3/4 t. summer savory
3/4 t. sweet basil
3/4 t. sweet marjoram
1/4 t. celery seed

Set the electric frying pan at 325° and fry the bacon until crisp but not brown. Remove bacon; drain on paper towels; pour off all but 2 T. of fat and add to it the butter. Saute the livers at 325°; reduce the temperature to 300° and cook until they are done all through. Force the warm livers through a coarse sieve and add remaining ingredients. Mix well and store in a covered container. Refrigerate several hours to ripen and before serving, allow to return to room temperature. This paté freezes well.

CHEESE WAFERS

1/4 lb. very sharp cheese, grated in a large *mouli*
1/4 c. butter or margarine
1/2 t. turmeric
1/4 t. salt
1/2 c. flour

Put all ingredients into a bowl, and allow to come to room temperature. Then work the mixture together with the hands until it is smooth and creamy. Roll out on a floured board and cut into fancy shapes appropriate to the season, hearts for St. Valentine's Day, hatchets for George Washington's birthday, shamrocks for St. Patrick's Day, eggs or chickens for Easter, turkeys for Thanksgiving, trees, bells and stars for Christmas.

Place on an ungreased aluminum cooky sheet (no Teflon) and bake in an oven preheated to 450° for from 5 to 7 minutes, depending upon thickness. Watch them, and turn when necessary. Cool, and store in a tight tin box.

SOUPS

MINESTRONE

It is fun to make this soup on a late September day when the sun is warm and you can find many of the ingredients in the garden. Pick them and save them from being taken by the first frost!

The ingredients:

2 smoked ham hocks
6 qts. water
1 lb. dried Roman beans (obtainable in Italian grocery stores)
1 qt. of chopped Savoy cabbage
1 c. mixed red and green sweet peppers
2 T. fat, skimmed from top of broth
1 1/2 c. Spanish or garden onions, measured after chopping
2 t. garlic, measured after putting through garlic press
1 young zucchini squash, about 7 inches long, cut up
6 c. fresh tomatoes, peeled, and most of the seeds removed
3 green onions with tops, sliced thin
1 1/2 c. squash blossoms, with tiny squashes attached, and new
    tips of squash leaves, cut up
1/2 c. celery, cut fine
1 1/2 t. fresh rosemary
2 T. sea salt
1/2 t. black pepper
1/8 t. ground allspice
1/4 c. fresh basil
1 T fresh French sorrel leaves
2 T. fresh parsley
1 T. fresh young chicory leaves
3 T. rice
2 T. barley
4 T. pasta "barley"
4 T. pasta "soupettes" called ditilini
3 T. alphabet noodles
1 T. white sugar
5 T. brown sugar
1 T. Angostura bitters

Directions: Wash the ham hocks, and put them on to cook in the 6 qts. of water. Simmer for 2 hours. Remove ham hocks, cool, and refrigerate. Strain the broth, cool and chill it. Remove the hard fat from the top of it and reserve 2 T. That night, soak the beans in enough water to amply cover them. In the morning, drain the beans and put them in the ham broth to cook. Simmer them until they are soft, from 1 1/2 to 2 hours. Cool them; put beans and broth through the Waring blender and then through a coarse sieve.

Melt the 2 T. of reserved ham fat in a frying pan and add to it the Spanish onions and the garlic. Cook over low heat until the onions are soft but not brown.

Add the contents of the frying pan to the soup kettle and then add all the other ingredients except the pastas. Bring to a boil, and cook, just barely bubbling, until the vegetables are done.

While the soup is simmering, cook the pastas in boiling salted water until almost done. Drain, and add them to the soup.

Trim the ham hocks, reserving all good meat, free from fat and gristle. Dice this meat, and add 2 cups of it to the soup when it is nearly done. Stir the soup well, finish the cooking and it is ready to serve or to freeze.

Serve it garnished with freshly grated Parmesan cheese, which is a different product from the canned grated Parmesan. Buy a pound, grate it, and store it in a covered jar in the freezer.

Minestrone can be made in winter by substituting canned for fresh tomatoes, some yellow squash for the squash blossoms and using your imagination for substitutes for the sorrel and the chicory.

WATERCRESS SOUP

2 T. butter
1 bunch watercress (1 1/2 c. firmly packed, measured after washing and removing heavy stems)
4 large shallots
1 qt. of rich, well-seasoned chicken stock (fat removed)

1 T. plus 2 t. cornstarch
1 c. milk, or cream, or half-and-half
salt and pepper

Melt butter, add watercress and shallots and simmer gently until watercress is wilted.

Put in the Waring blender, with one cup of stock. Blend. Combine this mixture with remaining broth and simmer 15 minutes. Mix the cornstarch with the milk, and stir until smooth. Add this to the stock and stir until thickened and smooth. Cream makes a prettier and better-flavored soup than milk, but milk is quite acceptable.

Keep the soup hot in a double boiler and correct the seasoning before serving.

Garnish with tiny buttered croûtons.

CLAM CHOWDER

3 slices bacon
3/4 c. chopped onion
1 c. diced celery
1 1/2 c. diced raw potato
1 c. water
1 t. dried celery leaves
1/2 t. thyme
3 c. milk
1 t. salt
A roux of 1 T. bacon fat and 1 T. flour, well blended
1 can minced clams (8 oz.) or the same amount of frozen minced clams
1 T. parsley

Fry bacon until crisp and dry in a heavy aluminum kettle; remove bacon and drain it on absorbent paper. Add onion to fat. Cook slowly, stirring until yellow. Drain off fat, reserving the T. for the roux. To the kettle, add celery, potatoes and water and seasonings. Simmer until vegetables are tender. Potato must hold its shape, so should not cook too long. Add clams, milk and crumbled bacon. Bring to boiling point but do not boil. Add roux; stir until it thickens; add the minced parsley and serve. May also be frozen.

YEAR'S END TURKEY SOUP
(from the carcass of a 25 lb. bird)

Remove all the meat from a cold roast turkey and store in a refrigerator. If there is a lot of stuffing left, save some of that and reserve it. Put all the remainder of the turkey into an 8-qt. kettle, all the bones, skin, fat—everything. Cover with cold water, add 2 large bay leaves and bring slowly to a boil. Simmer gently 4 hours. Strain the broth and remove any additional meat which the long cooking may have loosened from the bones. Add this to the meat already reserved; strain the broth and set in a cold place overnight.

Next morning, remove all the fat from the top of the broth and add the following:

8 single stalks of celery cut fine
3 medium-sized carrots, diced
3 medium-sized onions, chopped
2 T. white rice
1 1/2 T. pearl barley
1 T. yellow split peas and 1 T. green split peas
1 t. curry powder
1 large, whole peeled raw potato
10 ten-inch pieces of macaroni
Any leftover giblet gravy
2 or 3 c. of carefully trimmed and diced turkey meat

Bring to a boil. After 5 minutes, remove the macaroni with a skimmer. Cool it, and cut it, with scissors, into 1/4 inch pieces. Return it to the boiling soup. Simmer it gently for an hour; then mash the potato in the bottom of the kettle. Add turkey meat. Bring to a boil, mix thoroughly, and it is ready to serve or freeze. Garnish with minced parsley.

SORREL SOUP

2 T. butter
1/2 c. onion, cut up
1 c. fresh French sorrel, measured after washing, trimming and removing heavy ribs, firmly packed.
3 c. rich, well-seasoned chicken broth, fat removed
2 c. diced raw potatoes, boiled, in a minimum of water
1/2 c. heavy cream
1 T. cornstarch

Melt butter, add onion, and cook slowly until soft but not brown. Add the sorrel, the chicken broth, and the cooked potatoes with whatever water is left after cooking (not more than a cup).

Simmer 20 minutes.

Put the whole mixture through the Waring blender, 2 c. at a time. Reheat, and put through a coarse wire strainer. Mix the cornstarch with the cream and stir until smooth. Add it to the soup and stir until it thickens.

Serve garnished with minced parsley and tiny buttered croûtons.

CORN CHOWDER

4 slices lean bacon, diced (1/2 c.)
1/2 c. chopped onions
1 large or two medium-sized bay leaves
1 T. parsley, minced
1 3/4 t. salt
3 grindings black pepper
1 c. raw potatoes, diced

2 c. hot water

2 1/2 c. canned yellow corn, cream style, measured after straining
  through a coarse sieve

3/4 t. sage

3 T. flour

1/2 c. milk

2 c. milk

3 t. sugar

Fry the bacon in a heavy aluminum pot until it is crisp.
Remove bacon, drain on paper towels, then crumble fine.

Drain off all but 2 T. of the fat from the pan, then put in the
onions. Cook gently until soft. Do not brown.

Add bay leaf, parsley, salt, pepper and sage, potatoes, hot
water. Simmer the chowder until the potatoes are done, but still
hold their shape.

Now add the blended flour and milk and stir until the soup
thickens. Then add the strained crushed corn and the milk and
sugar and bacon. Mix thoroughly and pour the chowder into the
top of a double boiler. Cook over boiling water for 1/2 hr.
stirring now and then. Remove bay leaf, and serve the chowder
garnished with minced parsley or chives. The final cooking over
hot water improves the flavor of this hearty luncheon or supper
soup.

MEAT

ROAST LEG OF LAMB

I have promised several owners of the first edition that I would put this recipe for a roast of lamb in the new book without any changes. So here it is:

Six hours before dinner, put the leg of lamb in the roasting pan. Make three slits in the meat and insert in each one a leaf of rosemary. Rub the meat all over with a cut clove of garlic and squeeze over it the juice of one large lemon. Sprinkle over it 1 T. Hungarian paprika. Keep the meat at room temperature, basting, turning, getting the paprika and lemon juice well over and into the meat, so that by the time it goes into the oven it will be completely marinated. Three and a half hours before dinner, pour off the excess lemon juice, and put the meat into a 325° oven. Roast it for 3 1/4 hours, basting occasionally. During the last hour, reduce the temperature to 300°. Serve with a thin brown gravy made from the juices in the pan.

LAMB CROQUETTES

(from leftover roast of lamb; make sauce first)

THICK WHITE SAUCE

1/2 c. butter
1/2 c. flour
2 c. milk
1 1/2 t. salt
1/8 t. black pepper

Melt the butter in top of double boiler; add flour, mixing with a small wire whip. Add milk slowly stirring all the time until the mixture is thick and very smooth.

Measure 1 1/2 c. of this sauce to mix with the croquettes. Reserve the remainder as the basis of a sauce to serve with them.

The croquettes:

Cut all the meat from a cold roast leg of lamb. Trim carefully, removing all fat, skin and gristle. Grind the meat, using a medium knife in the meat grinder.

2 c. of this ground lamb, firmly packed.
1 T. freshly grated onion and juice
1 1/2 c. thick white sauce from preceding recipe
2 t. celery leaves, crumbled fine
1/4 t. thyme

Mix these ingredients thoroughly. Chill. Form into 12 croquettes. Dip these in seasoned crumbs, bread or cornflakes, then into beaten egg mixture (one large egg, 2 T. cold water, 1/4 t. salt) and then into crumbs again. After the croquettes have been dipped roll them on a board to make the sides smooth. Set them in the refrigerator until it is time to fry them in deep fat. At this point, they may be put into a tin box, with a tight lid, and frozen—to use weeks or months later. The basic sauce to serve with them may also be frozen and finished at the time the croquettes are used.

To fry the croquettes use a controlled heat electric saucepan with a wire basket. This takes the guess-work out of frying croquettes. Set the temperature at 380° and use enough peanut or corn oil to cover the croquettes in the basket; fry 2 or 3 at a time until they are nicely brown. Lift out in the basket and drain on paper towels. Frozen croquettes must be defrosted before frying. Serve the following sauce around the croquettes, not over them.

Sauce to serve with croquettes

1/2 c. or more of the thick white sauce (use all remaining from "Thick White Sauce" recipe)
1 c. milk
1/4 t. salt
1/2 c. cooked peas

Put the heavy sauce in a small saucepan over lowest heat, and add 1/4 c. of the milk. Stir now and then, and gradually add the remainder of the milk, stirring as it warms, with a wire whisk. It will come out satin smooth. Add the peas, mix well and serve. If the basic sauce has been frozen, let it defrost before using it in this recipe. Then set over low heat as described.

BEEF LOAF

1/2 c. milk	2 T. chopped onions
1 c. soft bread crumbs	1 T. celery leaves
1/4 c. wheat germ	1/2 t. summer savory
1 t. salt	1/4 t. French thyme
2 eggs, well beaten	1/4 t. sweet marjoram
1 1/2 lbs. ground round steak	1/4 t. sage
2 T. minced parsley	

Put the bread crumbs in a bowl, pour the milk over them, and stir until smooth. Add all the other ingredients, and mix well with the hands, until all is completely blended. Form into a loaf, and roll the loaf back and forth on a board until it is uniform in shape, and about 12 inches long. Put into a roasting pan, and pour over it 1/2 c. water. Bake in a 400° oven for 40 minutes, basting twice. Serve with a thin gravy made from the juices in the pan, or with mushroom sauce.

Mushroom Sauce

2 T. fat from the baking pan
1 c. coarsely chopped mushrooms
1 T. flour
1 c. water or stock or juices from the pan
salt

Put the fat into a saucepan, over medium heat. Add mushrooms, and cook slowly until they are soft. Add flour, and stir well. Then add water or stock; stir, as it comes to a boil. Simmer three minutes and serve. Leftover meat loaf may be sliced, put into a covered casserole with tomato sauce, and heated in the oven.

BAKED BEANS WITH PORK

1 lb. marrowfat beans	1/4 c. chili sauce
1/4 c. New Orleans molasses	1 t. dry mustard
1/4 c. dark Karo	1/2 t. rosemary
1/4 c. ketchup	1/2 t. summer savory
	2 t. salt

Small white onions, at least one for each person to be served. 2 lbs. fresh pork loin. This should either be boned, or have the bones sawed through so that in serving, it will be easy to separate the chops.

Cover the beans with cold water, late at night, as they need only a few hours soaking.

In the morning, drain and wash them, and put them in a kettle with the pork. Barely cover with water. Bring to a boil and simmer 1/2 hr. Remove the pork, and pour the beans and broth through a colander, saving the broth. Strain the broth through a fine strainer.

In an earthenware casserole mix all the seasonings with one cup of broth. Put the pork in the casserole, and then the beans. Bury the onions deep down in the beans, and add enough extra broth to come almost to the top of the beans. Save the remaining broth as it may be necessary to add some during the cooking.

Cover the casserole and put into a 300° oven. Bake from 9:00 A.M. until 12:30 P.M. Turn off the heat and let casserole remain in oven.

Halfway thru this cooking period, remove casserole from oven and gently stir the beans so as to get the seasonings evenly distributed. Push the onions down under the beans. Cover, and return to oven.

At 3:00 P.M. turn on the heat and set the temperature at 250°. Bake the casserole, covered, until 5:00 P.M. Remove cover, and bake, uncovered, until 6:00 P.M.

Serve with apple sauce or baked apples, Boston brown bread, and a green salad.

If Baked Beans are to be served at a buffet supper, the pork may be removed before the final baking, cut into inch-square chunks and mixed with the beans; then no carving will be necessary.

SAUSAGE

If you are a label reader, you may not like the list of ingredients which go into even good brands of commercial sausage and you may think it is worth the very small effort of making your own. The secret of producing a good, tender sausage seems to be, first of all, to start with a good piece of pork—a loin or a shoulder—which contains a good porportion of fat. The fat cooks out, but its presence when the sausage is made seems to insure that the sausage will be tender. So choose a fat piece of pork and do not trim off any of the fat.

3 lbs. fresh pork shoulder or loin. Have it ground once with a fine
 blade. Weight is after grinding.

2 t. black pepper	3/4 t. thyme
1/4 t. red pepper	1/2 t. summer savory
1 T. salt	1/2 t. sweet marjoram
1 1/2 t. sage	1/4 t. ground ginger

Put the meat in a large bowl, and sprinkle the seasonings on top. Work them in with the hands, taking plenty of time to get them well distributed. If the meat is very cold, it expedites the mixing to hold your hands under hot water once or twice. This recipe will make 25 patties. Wrap each one separately in plastic, and store them in a large container in the freezer.

PHILADELPHIA SCRAPPLE

Scrapple is a Philadelphia breakfast, but its popularity extends far beyond that city. If you do not like the list of ingredients on a package of commercial scrapple, try making your own. It is almost sure to taste better, and after you have made it once or twice, you will find that it is very little trouble.

Next to the quality of the pork, the most important ingredient in scrapple is the corn meal, of which there are many "grinds." There is the very fine, which is really a flour; the coarsest is called "corn grits." The right one for scrapple is a granulated meal, in between these two. The buckwheat flour should be the darkest you can find.

1 1/2 qts. water
1 lb. pork loin or shoulder, well streaked with fat (weight without bones)
1 c. yellow granulated corn meal
1/2 c. dark buckwheat flour
2 t. salt
1/4 t. black pepper
1 T. sage

Put the meat on to cook in the 1 1/2 qts. of water. Simmer for three hours. Remove meat, and strain broth. There should be 4 c. of broth. If there is more, reduce it; if there is less, add enough water to make 4 c.

Add all the seasonings to the broth and cool it. When cold, take out 1 1/2 c. of it and put in a bowl. Add to this the corn meal and the flour, in that order, a little at a time, stirring as you do so. If any lumps appear, stir with a large wire whisk until it is perfectly smooth. Heat the remaining broth and add to it gradually the corn meal mixture, stirring all the time. Use the wire whisk again if it shows a tendency to form lumps. After it is smooth, put on low heat for one hour, stirring occasionally. At the end of the hour, add the meat, which has been prepared as follows: trim off any skin or gristle, but save every bit of fat. Chop it fine in a wooden chopping bowl.

After adding the pork to the kettle, cook and stir for 15 minutes more. Then pour the scrapple into a standard-size bread pan, 9 by 5 by 2 3/4 inches.

Cool, then chill, and let stand in the refrigerator at least overnight before slicing.

To fry scrapple

Run a knife around the sides of the pan to loosen the scrapple, and turn upside down on a bread board. Hold a cloth wrung out of very hot water on the bottom of the pan, and it will fall out easily. Set the electric frying pan at 350°. Using a very sharp knife with a serrated edge, cut the scrapple in 1/2 inch slices. Flour each slice on both sides. Put 2 or 3 T. of peanut or corn oil in the pan and when it is hot, lay the slices in it. It should cook rather slowly, so as to develop a crisp brown crust. When brown on both sides, drain on paper towels and serve. Horseradish and buttered toast are good with it.

SAVORY STUFFING FOR TURKEY, CHICKEN OR DOUBLE PORK CHOPS

This amount will stuff a 28-lb. bird.

5 1/2 qts. (22 c.) soft, fresh bread crumbs
8 medium-sized onions, chopped
8 stalks celery, cut into tiny pieces
1 1/4 c. melted butter (no substitute)

1/2 t. black pepper	2 T. sweet marjoram
1/2 t. white pepper	2 T. sage
3 T. minced parsley	1 t. French thyme
1 t. summer savory	2 T. salt

Crumble the bread fine with the hands. This will take an hour. If you haven't an hour, the crumbs can be made in a jiffy in one of the newer blenders. However, the handmade crumbs make a better stuffing. The crumbs should be of the consistency of brown sugar.

Measure the crumbs, add all the seasonings, except the butter, and then mix well with the hands. Then add the butter and mix again until the whole is completely blended. Stuff the turkey lightly. The stuffing should not be packed too firmly, and yet the bird should be well-filled. Any that is left, can be frozen for use at a later date; it will keep a long time.

FISH

BAKED HADDOCK

4 fillets of haddock, for individual servings
1 onion
4 leaves of fresh sweet basil or 1 t. dried basil
1 T. fresh lemon juice
Salt, paprika, minced parsley
1/2 c. thin white sauce
1 large bay leaf

Butter a shallow baking dish, and lay the four servings of fish on it. Slip under each fillet a slice of onion, one leaf of fresh basil and a bit of bay leaf. Put a few drops of lemon juice on each piece of fish and sprinkle with salt. Spread the white sauce on the tops also. The sauce should cover the entire surface, leaving almost none to run off. Bake 20 minutes in a 375° oven. Serve in the baking dish. The onion, bay leaf and basil are for seasoning only, and should not be served with the fish. Before serving, sprinkle with minced parsley.

Thin white sauce

1 1/2 t. butter	1/4 t. salt
1 1/2 t. flour	1 grinding black pepper
1/2 c. milk	Minced parsley

Melt the butter, stir in the flour, and add the milk gradually. Cook gently until it thickens; let the sauce cool a little while, and then pour it over the fillets, trying, as you do so, to keep it all on top of the fish.

CASSEROLE OF SCALLOPS

4 T. butter
1/2 lb. button mushrooms (if large, cut up)
4 T. flour
2 c. milk

3/4 t. salt
1/8 t. pepper
1 lb. bay scallops (if sea scallops, cut up into bite size pieces)
1/4 t. each: French thyme, basil, sweet marjoram, summer
    savory, dried celery leaves
3/4 c. finely diced fresh celery
1 c. buttered, seasoned soft bread crumbs for the top

Crumbs for the top

1 c. soft, fresh bread crumbs
2 T. melted butter
1/4 t. salt
1/2 t. French thyme
1/2 t. sweet basil
Mix well.

Melt butter; add mushrooms, washed but not peeled. (Cut a thin slice from the base of each stem.) Cook gently a few minutes, stirring. Add flour, then milk, stirring constantly until the mixture thickens. Add remaining ingredients and pour into a buttered casserole. Sprinkle with the prepared bread crumbs.

Put the casserole into a 350° oven and bake for 40 minutes. Serve with something crisp, like drop baking powder biscuits, baked in muffin tins, which have a delicious crisp crust.

QUICK FILLETS OF SOLE

Butter a shallow French pottery baking dish and lay on it the number of fillets needed. Pour over them some dry sauterne, enough so that the bottom of the dish is covered and a little lies around the fish. Season with salt, a few grindings of pepper and sprinkle parsley, chervil and chives on top of the fillets, so that they look green. Sprinkle with blanched, silvered almonds. Put into a 450° oven and bake for 10 minutes.

SHRIMP NEWBURG

This is a nice change from shrimp with ketchupy sauces, especially in summer when good fresh tomatoes are on the menu all the time.

1 lb. medium-sized shrimp cooked in court bouillon according to directions and cleaned; there should be 2 c.

2 T. butter	3/4 t. sugar
1 3/4 T. flour	1/2 t. salt
1 c. light cream	3 T. sherry
3 T. fresh lemon juice	1/8 t. paprika

Melt butter in the top of a double boiler; add flour and cream gradually. Stir with a wire whisk until satin smooth. Add seasonings and stir to blend. Add the cooked shrimp and cook until very hot. Serve in a rice ring. Serves four.

Court bouillon for shrimp

2 qts. water	4 whole cloves
4 or 5 celery tops	1/2 t. cracked black pepper
1 carrot, sliced but not peeled	1 T. salt
2 onions	2 T. vinegar
1 bay leaf	

Bring to a boil, drop in the shrimp, and simmer 20 minutes from the time the bouillon comes to a boil again. Let the shrimp cool in the bouillon; then remove shells and intestinal veins. They are then ready to use in this recipe.

EGGS

SHIRRED EGGS

I grew up in a household which boasted of two sizes of "egg-shirrers," a one-egg and a two-egg size. The former is no longer available, but a Pyrex dish, which is called an "individual pie plate," can be bought, which will take care of either one or two eggs. It has the advantage of being inexpensive, in comparison with the china dish. The pyrex dish is shallow, like a pie plate, with sloping sides.

Butter this dish, and crumble in the bottom of it one slice of crisply cooked bacon. Sprinkle over it one medium-sized shallot, sliced. Drop in two eggs; pour one t. cream over each egg, add salt, and a pinch of each of two dried herbs, evenly distributed over the top. Basil and summer savory are good, or sweet marjoram and lovage. Over it, grate some fresh Parmesan or cheddar cheese. Put into a 300° oven, and bake for 10 or 15 minutes depending upon how soft you like your eggs. If you do not like cheese for breakfast, as I do, omit it, and use the cheese some day when you have Shirred Eggs for luncheon.

DEVILLED SCRAMBLED EGGS

6 eggs	1/2 t. salt
1/2 c. thick sour cream	1/4 t. pepper
1 t. herb-flavored mustard	2 T. butter

Stir the mustard into the sour cream. Break the eggs into a mixer bowl, and beat them. Add the cream and mustard, salt and pepper, using the lowest speed. Melt the butter in an electric frying pan, set at 275°, and pour eggs into it. Stir gently as it cooks. Serve garnished with 2 bacon curls, a tiny bunch of watercress and 3 peeled cherry tomatoes for each person. To peel the tomatoes, drop tomatoes into boiling water 1 minute. Drain and place under running water until cold. Peel.

EGG TIMBALES WITH BREAD SAUCE

6 eggs
1 t. salt
1/2 t. pepper

1 t. grated onion and juice
2 t. chives, fresh or frozen,
    cut fine
1 1/2 c. milk

Make bread sauce first.

Beat the eggs without separating; add seasonings and milk. Mix well, and pour into well-buttered timbale moulds. Bake, surrounded by hot water, in a 325° oven. Begin to test them at the end of 30 minutes. If a knife comes out clean, they are done. Remove them from the hot water the instant they are firm, and unmould on a hot platter and surround with BREAD SAUCE.

BREAD SAUCE

1 c. soft fresh bread crumbs from center of loaf
1 onion, into which 5 cloves have been pushed
1/2 t. salt
1 t. paprika
1/2 t. dried basil, powdered
1 pint milk
Make crumbs fine before measuring

Put all ingredients in top of double boiler, set over boiling water and cook one hour. Remove onion and cloves; add butter. Beat well, and pour around, not over, the timbales. Garnish the whole with a half cup of coarse bread crumbs, which have been browned in the oven, with 2 T. butter. This crisp, brown garnish is important to the success of the dish.

TARRAGON BREAKFAST SOUFFLE

2 T. butter
2 t. chopped shallot
4 large eggs
1 1/3 c. milk

3/4 t. salt
1/8 t. pepper
1 1/2 t. tarragon

Put the butter in the top of a double boiler, and set it over boiling water. Add the shallots.

Beat the eggs in the mixer, add the milk, salt and pepper. Stir in the tarragon by hand.

Stir the butter and shallots, and pour the egg mixture into the top of the double boiler. Cover it, and cook over boiling water for 20 minutes. This will serve four.

STRAWBERRY OMELET # 1

4 eggs, separated
1 T. plus 1 t. 10X sugar
1 T. plus 1 t. flour
1 T. plus 1 t. cream
1/4 t. salt
6 T. Alpine strawberries, fresh or frozen. If frozen, allow them to defrost to the point where berries can be separated.
2 T. butter (salted)

Beat the egg whites until stiff, and set aside. Then beat the yolks until thick and creamy, and add to them the sugar, salt, flour and cream. Beat again. Fold the whites gently into the yolks, and add the berries, mixing carefully by hand. Put the butter into a 9 1/2-inch iron frying pan (top measurement) and 1 7/8 inch deep and set over high heat for a minute, until butter is melted. Roll butter around to coat the sides of pan also. Then pour in the omelet mixture, and remove from the heat at once. Put the pan into a 325° oven and bake for 10 minutes, until lightly brown on top. Remove from oven, fold the omelet, transfer to a hot platter, dust with powdered sugar and garnish with bacon curls.

STRAWBERRY OMELET # 2

Use the same ingredients, omitting the Alpine strawberries in the omelet mixture. When you remove the omelet from the oven, spread 1/2 of it with 4 T. slightly warm strawberry jam, and fold. Garnish the platter with 1/2 to 1 c. of Alpine strawberries, fresh or frozen. If frozen, they should be almost completely defrosted.

BREAD

NELDA'S HERB BREAD

1 cake yeast
1/4 c. lukewarm water
1 t. sugar
2 c. milk
1/4 c. butter
1/2 c. sugar
1 1/4 t. salt

1 1/4 t. sage
1 1/4 t. freshly ground nutmeg
4 t. caraway seed, whole
2 well-beaten eggs
6 1/2 c. flour, s.b.m.
1/2 c. flour on the bread
    board for kneading

Combine the first three ingredients and set aside. Scald milk; add butter, sugar and salt. Cool to lukewarm and add sage, nutmeg and caraway. Stir, and add the yeast mixture and 2 c. of the flour. Beat well; cover and let rise until light and bubbly. Add eggs, remaining flour, and mix with the hands. Let rise, covered until very light; then knead on a floured bread board until the dough is springy, and creases disappear at once. Let rise again.

When doubled in bulk, divide into five balls, then form into five loaves for pans which measure 6 inches by 3 1/4 inches at the top, and are 2 1/4 inches deep. Butter the pans well, and let the loaves rise until they are nearly doubled in bulk. Then brush the tops with melted butter, and let rise a few minutes longer. Put the loaves on the top shelf of a 350° oven and bake for 30 minutes. Remove from oven; cool on a wire rack.

CARDAMOM BREAD

2 yeast cakes
1/2 c. lukewarm water + 1 t. sugar
1 c. milk
1 1/4 t. salt
1 c. sugar
3/4 c. soft butter (no substitute)
1 T. finely crushed cardamom seeds (Shell, remove kernels, pound them fine with a mortar and pestle.) Measure after crushing.

3 eggs, well-beaten in a mixer
6 c. unbleached flour, s.b.m., and a little extra for kneading.

Dissolve yeast in warm water; add 1 t. sugar. Scald the milk; add salt, 1/2 c. of the sugar, the cardamom and the butter. Mix well. When it is lukewarm add the yeast mixture and 2 c. of the flour. Cover and let rise. When it is very light, add the eggs and the remaining 1/2 c. of sugar, and the remaining 4 c. of flour. Put dough on a lightly floured board, and knead until the dough is elastic, and the creases disappear at once. Let rise again. When it is light, punch down. Let rise until doubled in bulk.

Return to the board, and form into four loaves; put into pans that measure 6 by 3 1/4 inches at the top and are 2 1/4 inches deep. Butter the pans heavily, and put the bread in them, spreading the dough with the hands, so that it reaches the corners. Let the bread rise in a warm place, covered. Do not let it quite double in bulk this time, or it will be coarse in texture. It rises tremendously in the oven.

When light, put it into a 375° oven, and bake at that temperature for 10 minutes. Reduce the heat to 350° and bake 30 minutes longer.

DILLY CASSEROLE BREAD

1/4 c. lukewarm water
1 t. sugar
1 yeast cake
1 c. lukewarm cottage cheese
2 T. sugar
2 T. minced white onion

1 T. soft butter
1 T. dill seed
1 t. salt
1/4 t. soda
2 eggs, well-beaten
2 c. flour, s.b.m.

Combine the first three ingredients, and set aside. In a large bowl, combine the warm cottage cheese, the sugar, onion, butter, dill seed, salt and soda.

Mix well, and add the yeast mixture.

Stir until blended, and add one cup of the flour. Beat well, and set in a warm place to rise.

When very light, add the eggs, mix with the hands, cover the bowl, and let rise again.

When doubled in bulk, pour batter into a well-buttered 2-qt. 8-inch glass casserole, and let rise again until very light.

Sprinkle the top of the loaf with coarse salt.

Then set the casserole on the top shelf of a 350° oven, and bake for 45 minutes, covering the loaf with aluminum foil for the last 15 minutes.

Remove from oven, and cool in the casserole. When almost cold, cut the bread into wedge-shaped pieces. It must be warmed a few minutes in a hot oven before serving. It freezes well, and by cutting it before it is frozen, it is easy to remove the number of pieces needed. It is a good luncheon or supper bread, and is best with unsalted butter.

PAIN d' EPICE

One of the numerous culinary specialties of Dijon, that gastronomic center of France, is pain d' epice, a wonderful spice bread which comes in several incarnations, plain and fruited.

When we were traveling around that lovely French countryside near Dijon, pain d'epice was always included in our picnic lunches.

The following recipe for a plain spice bread is better, I think, than any we had in Dijon.

2 eggs
1/2 c. sugar
1 T. baking soda
1 c. hot, not boiling, water
1 c. honey
1 1/2 t. ground cinnamon
1 1/4 t. anise seed, pounded in a mortar
1/4 t. salt
1 T. cognac
1 1/2 c. stone ground rye flour
1 c. Ceresota flour

1 1/2 t. grated orange rind
Brown sugar for pans
Set the oven at 350°

Beat eggs in a large mixer bowl. Add sugar, soda and hot water (the latter very slowly), beating as you do so, then honey and flavorings. Beat rather fast while you butter the pan; then add the flours, a little at a time, continuing to beat.

This recipe will just fill a pan which measures 11 1/2 by 4 1/2 by 2 1/2 inches. It should be buttered thickly. Shake brown sugar into the buttered pan, tipping it back and forth to coat it evenly. Shake out most of the excess. Then shake flour into the pan, and coat it lightly all over.

Pour the batter into the pan, pushing it up against the sides, because the loaf has a tendency to rise high in the center. Set oven at 350°. Bake 45 minutes and remove carefully from the pan, loosening the sides with a knife. Cool on a wire rack, in the same position it occupied in the pan—topside up. With this sugar and flour treatment the bread does not stick. While it is still warm, move it gently on the wire rack so that it will not stick to the rack. Serve plain or with unsalted butter.

KULICH
(An authentic Russian Easter Bread)

2 cakes of yeast
1/2 c. lukewarm water
2 t. sugar
1 t. salt
1 3/4 c. milk, scalded and cooled to lukewarm
1 c. sugar
1 c. flour, s.b.m.
6 egg yolks
1/2 c. sugar
1 1/2 c. sweet butter, melted very gently
7 c. flour, s.b.m.
1/4 lb. seedless raisins

126

Kulich

Biscuit
Tortoni

1/4 lb. blanched, toasted, chopped almonds
1/2 lb. mixed candied fruits, cherries, citron, orange and lemon
 peel.
1/2 t. saffron
2 T. brandy
12 cardamom seeds
1 whole vanilla bean
            or
1 t. powdered vanilla, Ste. Marie brand
3 egg whites, stiffly beaten

Dissolve the yeast cakes in the warm water, and add the 2 t.
sugar.

Add to the milk the salt, 1 c. sugar, yeast mixture, and the
flour. Let rise, covered, until very light.

Beat the egg yolks with the 1/2 cup of sugar, and stir them into
the risen dough. Add the butter, very slowly, and the 7 c. flour.
Soak the saffron in the brandy for ten minutes, strain the
infusion and add it. Shell the cardamom seeds, and pound the
kernels in a mortar until they are a powder. Scrape the inside
from the vanilla bean and add that with the cardamom. Add the
fruits and incorporate them in the dough. Flour the bread board,
and knead the dough until it is smooth and the creases disappear
at once. Then add the stiffly beaten egg whites and work them
into the mixture. Let rise again, until very light. Then divide the
dough into four even pieces, and work them into 4 smooth balls;
put each ball into a thickly buttered, one pound coffee can,
which measures 5 1/2 inches in height by 4 inches in diameter.
Let rise again. Bake the four coffee cans in an oven preheated to
350° for 40 minutes. Remove from cans to wire racks. Cool the
loaves on their sides, not upright, as they tend to lean like the
Tower of Pisa in an upright position. Gently roll them back and
forth as they cool. When cold, stand upright, and ice the tops
with confectioner's sugar icing, letting it dribble down the sides
but not cover them.

When the icing has set, and is cold, insert a pretty fresh or
artificial flower in the top of the loaf, and slice it horizontally,

removing the top slice first to use as a lid. If it is not all used, replace the top slice and the loaf looks pretty until next time.

Kulich freezes successfully, and always makes a lovely gift at holiday time. It is so good that its use should not be limited to Easter.

Icing

1 1/2 c. confectioner's sugar
4 T. hot milk

Mix with a wire whisk until smooth. Cool and spread on tops of Kulich allowing it to drop down the sides. Kulich is good with morning coffee, or with afternoon tea or for a festive breakfast.

A FRESH HERB LOAF

1 yeast cake
1/4 c. lukewarm water with 1 t. sugar
1/2 c. hot water
1/4 c. sugar
3 T. butter
1 t. salt
1/3 c. fresh orange juice or undiluted frozen juice (thawed)
3 c. unbleached flour, s.b.m.
1 egg, well-beaten
1 t. grated orange rind
1/3 c. minced parsley
1/3 c. chives, cut fine
1/4 c. fresh tarragon, finely cut

Dissolve yeast in the warm water. Pour the hot water into a bowl; add the sugar, butter, salt and orange juice, in that order.

Stir until butter is melted and sugar dissolved, and then add to it the yeast mixture. Beat well. Add 1 c. of the flour and stir until smooth. Cover the bowl, and let rise in a warm place until it is very light.

Then add the egg, orange rind and herbs, and 1 1/2 c. of the flour, saving the remaining 1/2 c. to use on the bread board for kneading. Let rise again until light, and then knead the dough until it is smooth and the creases disappear quickly. Cover, and let rise again. When light, punch down and let rise again. When it is again light, turn out on the board and form into one large loaf for a standard size bread pan, or in two loaves, to fit two pans which measure 7 1/4 by 3 1/2 by 2 1/4. I like the two small pans better.

Butter the pans generously, and put the loaves in them, and let rise until very light. The dough can rise above the top of the pan and the bread will not be coarse. Set the oven at 350°.

Bake the single large loaf for 40 minutes, then reduce the heat to 325° and bake 10 minutes longer.

Bake the small loaves at 350° for 30 minutes, turn off the heat, and let remain in the oven 10 minutes longer.

Ten minutes before the bread is done, brush the tops with melted butter. Remove from pans and cool on a rack.

BEVERAGES

QUICK HERB-FLAVORED TOMATO JUICE

1 can unseasoned tomato juice (1 qt. 14 oz.)
2 t. basil
1 t. dried celery leaves
2 bay leaves
1/2 t. fresh rosemary
2 t. horseradish (prepared)
2 T. sugar
1 medium-sized white onion, sliced

Combine ingredients in a two-quart glass jar, cover, shake, and stand in the refrigerator overnight. Strain first through a coarse strainer, then through a fine strainer; chill until it is to be used.

MIDWINTER PUNCH FOR TWELVE

2 quarts and 1 c. of water
The following dried herbs:
3/4 c. sweet woodruff
1 T. black peppermint
2 T. spearmint
3 T. lemon verbena
1 c. lemon juice
1 c. and 1 T. sugar
1 T. grated orange rind (a navel orange)
2 c. apricot nectar
1 c. fresh orange juice
1 large navel orange, divided into sections free from membrane, and each section cut into small pieces
1 c. frozen Alpine strawberries

Drop the herbs into the water, and bring to a rolling boil. Remove at once from heat, cover, and steep 10 minutes. Strain through a very fine strainer or a piece of wet cheesecloth. Add 1 c. of sugar, stir until dissolved, and cool. Mash the orange rind into the extra T. of sugar, and add that, then the lemon juice, the orange juice and the apricot nectar. Let stand in a cold place until shortly before serving time, and then add the orange and the strawberries, the latter still frozen.

Put an ice ring in the punch bowl, and pour the punch over it.

MIDWINTER ICE RING

Pour cold water into a ring mould to the depth of one inch. Freeze hard. Remove from freezer, and lay on the ice, in a pattern, the leaves and flowers of rose geranium, crowfoot geranium, and nutmeg geranium—any or all of them, whichever are available. Another pretty ring is decorated with the flowers and leaves of the trailing rosemary, and if you have a star jasmine in bloom, that is pretty too. Cover the leaves and flowers with a small amount of water, remembering as you arrange the leaves, that the mould will be reversed in the punch bowl. Freeze the mould again. When frozen hard, fill the mould with water, and put it back in the freezer for the final freezing.

A MAI BOWLE

For each bottle of white wine of your own choice, use 4 T. dried sweet woodruff. Put the herb into a bowl, and cover it with one bottle of wine. Place it, tightly covered, in the refrigerator over night. Strain it into a punch bowl, using a coarse strainer first, then a fine tea strainer. Add the rest of the wine, which has been well chilled, and stir it well.

For each bottle of wine, add to the punch bowl one t. brandy and 1 T. crushed strawberries, and mix again.

Serve with a strawberry and a sprig of fresh sweet woodruff in each punch cup.

THE MORAVIAN MAI BOWLE

6 c. water
1 c. dried sweet woodruff, firmly packed
1 1/2 c. fresh strawberries (not Alpines)

1 T. grated orange rind
1 T. grated lemon rind
1 c. sugar
2 c. fresh orange juice
1 1/4 c. fresh lemon juice
3 c. canned apricot nectar

Drop the sweet woodruff into the boiling water, and allow to steep (removed from heat) for ten minutes. Strain, first through a coarse strainer, then through a fine tea strainer, and add to the tea the sugar. Stir until dissolved. Cool it, and add the remaining ingredients. Mix well.

This Mai Bowle may be served at once, or refrigerated for a few hours, or frozen.

At serving time, pour it into a punch bowl, and put an ice ring in it to chill it. In the center of the ring, put a bunch of fresh sweet woodruff with its blossoms, and outside the ring, put in about a cup of Alpine strawberries. Serve in punch cups, with strawberries in each cup.

THE ICE RING

Choose an aluminium ring mould which will fit your punch bowl. A fluted ring is pretty. Pour some water into the mould, to a depth of one inch. Freeze it.

Remove from freezer, and lay on the ice a design in the leaves and flowers of sweet woodruff, remembering that in serving, the ring will be reversed. Cover the design with enough water to hold it in place, and freeze again, until very hard.

Remove from freezer, and lay on the ice a design in Alpine strawberries. Cover them carefully with water, and return to freezer. When frozen hard, remove from freezer and add enough water to fill the mould. Return to freezer and freeze hard.

ORANGE-SPICE TEA

1 lb. the best orange pekoe tea
1 c. dried orange peel

3 T. cinnamon stick, cracked into small pieces with a mortar and pestle
2 T. cracked whole cloves
6 T. dried lemon verbena leaves, cut up with scissors

Mix well, and store in jars. This amount will fill 7 eight-ounce jars (size of jar—not weight of tea).

To prepare orange peel: Peel California navel oranges with carrot peeler. Cut these strips of peel into fine shreds with sharp scissors. Spread out on cookie sheets and put in a warm place to dry. This may take several days.

In brewing this tea, use a scant teaspoon to a cup, maybe less. It develops more flavor than orange pekoe alone. Never serve milk or cream with this tea—use honey and lemon.

MISCELLANEOUS

MINT SAUCE FOR LAMB

2 T. minced fresh spearmint
1 rounded t. sugar
2 T. spearmint vinegar
1 T. water
1/8 t. salt

Mix the sugar with the mint, crushing out the juice with a spoon. Add the other ingredients, stirring until sugar and salt are dissolved. Serve with roast lamb or lamb chops.

MINT SHERBET

This is a tart, refreshing sherbet to accompany dinner. If sometime you should want to use it for dessert, it should be made a little sweeter.

1 t. unflavored gelatine
2 T. cold water
1 c. water
1/2 c. dried herb-peppermint or spearmint
1/2 c. sugar
1/2 c. orange juice
1/4 c. lemon juice
4 drops green coloring
2 egg whites, beaten very stiff

Soak gelatine in the cold water. Put water in a saucepan and drop the herb into it. Bring to a boil; remove from heat; cover and let steep 10 minutes. Strain through a coarse and then a fine strainer. Add the gelatine to the hot tea—and then the sugar. Stir until sugar is dissolved. Cool. Add fruit juices and green coloring. Pour into a shallow pan and set it in the freezer or the freezing compartment of refrigerator. When partially frozen, take from freezer, put into a bowl, and beat well. Add the egg whites; beat again. Then return to the freezer.

When it is again frozen—not too hard—remove from freezer and put into the bowl of the electric mixer, and beat until smooth. Return to the pan, cover tightly with aluminum foil, and return to the freezer until needed.

SAVORY RICE

2 T. chopped white onions
3 T. butter
1 c. white rice, well washed and drained
1 t. salt
1 t. dried summer savory
1 t. dried sweet marjoram
2 t. fresh or frozen parsley
2 t. fresh or frozen chives
1 t. fresh or frozen chervil
3 c. well-seasoned chicken stock

Melt butter in a heavy aluminum pot, add onions, and cook gently, stirring, for about five minutes. Add the rice, seasonings and chicken stock. Mix well. Cover the pot, and cook over low heat until the liquid is absorbed, stirring with a fork once or twice. This will take about a half-hour.

HERB-FLAVORED MUSTARD

This mustard is always made in summer, with fresh herbs. Only the Greek oregano is dry, because I have never grown an oregano which has as good a flavor as the imported wild marjoram from Greece.

This is a large recipe because I made it in quantities for church bazaars. It was as popular an item as the poppy seed dressing. The recipe can easily be halved or quartered if you like. As it stands, it fills 24 four-ounce jars.

1 gallon Gulden's prepared mustard, Dijon style. (This can be procured from a wholesale house.) If you cannot find it: Brown

mustard is better than yellow. Avoid "salad style" mustards. The Dijon style is best.

3 1/2 T. celery seed
6 T. sweet basil
3/4 c. summer savory
3 T. sweet marjoram
3 T. French thyme
4 T. sugar
4 T. dry sherry
1 T. Greek oregano (dry)
2 c. chives

Put all the herbs except the chives and the oregano through the little *mouli persil*, one at a time, measuring after grinding. Cut the chives into tiny bits with sharp scissors, and crumble the oregano.

Mix all ingredients, and let the mustard stand in a large, covered container for a few days, for flavors to blend, before putting it in small jars.

HERB BUTTER

For tea sandwiches, broiled fish and sometimes hamburgers.

To 1/4 lb. of butter (room temperature) add the following fresh herbs:
2 t. parsley
2 t. chives and the following dried herbs
1 t. basil
1 t. sweet marjoram
1 t. French thyme

After mixing the herbs and the butter, let it stand in a covered jar, in a warm room for an hour or two for the flavors to blend.

Use for open tea sandwiches on thin white bread, always bringing it to room temperature before spreading it. Refrigerate or freeze.

CARROTS WITH TARRAGON

2 1/2 c. young carrots, peeled and sliced thin crosswise
2 T. butter
2 T. boiling water
1 t. sugar
2 to 4 big green leaves of lettuce
2 or 3 grindings of pepper
1 scant t. salt
1 t. minced parsley
1/4 t. dry tarragon or 1/2 t. fresh tarragon minced
2 T. sweet cream

Put all ingredients except cream into a heavy aluminum pot. Cover. Simmer forty-five minutes, stirring two or three times. When ready to serve, add the cream and stir gently with a fork.

SALAD DRESSINGS

POPPY-SEED DRESSING

Whenever this dressing has appeared at bazaars of the Central Moravian Church, it has caused a modest sensation. People who have had it for the first time will ask me, in church, at a symphony concert, or just on the telephone, how they can get another bottle. It is good with a bowl of mixed lettuces, or on any fruit salad, and I have never known anyone who did not like it. Even grandchildren with the most finical appetites gratefully accept a bottle of it as a gift.

This is the first publication of this recipe, which I usually make in larger quantities, so as to have some on hand for gifts. It will keep a long time in the refrigerator, but that will not be one of your concerns.

1/2 c. sugar
1 t. dry mustard
1 t. paprika
1 t. salt
2 T. chopped onion
1/3 c. cider vinegar
2 T. unstrained lemon juice, seeds removed
1/3 c. strained honey
1 c. peanut or other oil (never olive oil)
1 1/2 T. poppy seed

Put sugar, mustard, paprika, salt, onion, vinegar, lemon juice in the Waring blender. Blend briefly, and transfer contents of the blender to a mixing bowl. Add honey and oil, and beat until smooth. Add poppy-seed, and mix thoroughly by hand. Store in covered container in refrigerator. Always bring to room temperature before using, and shake well.

PANSY'S SALAD DRESSING

3/4 c. sugar
1 T. flour

1 t. salt
1 1/2 t. prepared mustard
1/2 c. chives blossom vinegar
3/4 c. cream, sweet or sour, or evaporated milk
2 eggs, well-beaten
1 t. celery seed

Mix dry ingredients in the top of a double boiler. Add remaining ingredients, beat well, and cook over boiling water, stirring constantly until mixture thickens. Remove from heat, cool and chill. Stir once in a while as it cools.

It may be used for many salads just this way, but for a salad of mixed greens, it is better to thin it with a little cream.

LOU DENISE'S FRUIT SALAD DRESSING

4 egg yolks
4 T. sugar
4 T. tarragon vinegar
1/2 pt. heavy cream, whipped

Beat the egg yolks until thick and smooth, add sugar and vinegar and beat again. Cook over boiling water until the mixture thickens, stirring constantly. When thick, remove from heat, cool and chill. Add the whipped cream, and mix gently.

Winter salad
1 slice canned pineapple
1/2 canned pear
1 section of navel orange

Summer salad
Strawberries
Black cherries
Fresh pineapple

For a "Soup, Salad and Dessert" luncheon, the following is a good main-dish salad, served with Lou's Dressing.

Individual serving

Small lettuce cups, filled with
1. Dates stuffed with walnuts, and cut in crosswise slices
2. Fresh pineapple cubes, dipped in sugared minced fresh spearmint
3. Melon balls
4. Orange and grapefruit sections, membrane removed
5. Balls of cream cheese, dusted with paprika

QUICK SOUR CREAM DRESSING

3 T. thick sour cream
1 T. herb-flavored vinegar of your choice
1 T. sugar
1/4 t. salt

Mix well, and serve on lettuce or on mixed greens. Serves two.

DORIC HOUSE SALAD DRESSING

This dressing, which breaks all the rules for using herbs, was popular at the old Doric House, of fond memory, at Flemington, New Jersey. It always appeared on the same salad, made of pineapple and chunks of Roquefort cheese.

2 T. sugar	1 t. anise seed
2 t. salt	2/3 c. tarragon malt vinegar
1/4 t. pepper	1 pint olive oil
1/8 t. dry mustard	2 T. Worcestershire sauce
1 t. sweet paprika	Dash of tabasco sauce
1 t. dill seed	2 1/2 T. fresh lemon juice
1 t. tarragon	1 clove garlic or one whole onion
1 t. fennel seed	

Mix herbs, sugar, salt and pepper with the vinegar. Add olive oil, and beat well. Add remaining ingredients, beat again, and pour into a jar. Keep refrigerated, but always bring to room temperature before serving. Shake well before using.

ASSORTED SWEETS

CUMIN SEED COOKIES

3/4 c. butter
1 c. sugar
1 large egg
2 t. baking powder
1/4 c. heavy cream
1 T. cumin seed, pounded in a mortar
1 1/2 c. flour, s.b.m.
2 t. whole cumin seed, mixed with 2 t. granulated sugar, for tops
of cookies

Cream the butter and sugar until fluffy; add the egg, and beat again. Stir the cumin seed into the mixture by hand; then add the flour and baking powder which have been sifted together. Knead with the hands until well blended.

Roll out the dough on a lightly floured board, and cut out with a floured cooky cutter. Decorate the tops with the seed and sugar mixture, and put on a buttered aluminum cooky sheet in a 375° oven. Bake for about 15 minutes, watching them, until the edges are brown. This recipe makes 115 one-and-three-quarter-inch cookies. The flavor is improved by letting them stand in a covered tin box for a day or two before serving them.

BENNE SEED WAFERS [Sesame seed]

2 eggs, separated
1 c. brown sugar
5/8 c. sesame seed, toasted
1/4 t. salt
6 T. flour (5/8 c.)
Oven—350°

In the large mixer bowl, beat the whites of the eggs until stiff; in the small bowl, beat the yolks. Add to the yolks the sugar, salt, and flour, using the slowest speed for the flour. Stir in the sesame seed by hand, and then lightly fold in the egg whites.

Using a teaspoon in each hand, drop the cookies from the tip of a teaspoon onto a well-buttered aluminum cooky sheet (not Teflon), leaving two inches between them. Bake until the cookies are brown, the edges a little darker than the center. This will take about 9 minutes. If the cookies stick, wipe off the spatula with a paper towel. When these wafers are just done, they neither wrinkle nor stick, and a little experience is all that is needed to judge which is the magic moment to remove them from the pan. This recipe makes 112 small wafers. Store in an air-tight jar or tin can.

To toast sesame seed:

Spread the seeds on a flat aluminum pan and put into a 300° oven. In 10 minutes, stir the seeds, and return to oven. Repeat this several times, until the seeds are a nice, even, light brown. This may take 1/2 hour. Remove from oven, cool, and they are ready to use in these cookies.

FRESH FRUIT CUP

Use sections of pink and also yellow grapefruit and California oranges, taken out whole; seeded halves of Emperor and Malaga grapes; small chunks of D'Anjou pears; fresh pineapple and balls of any melons that are in the market or in the freezer. Sweeten to taste, keeping it on the tart side, and for the amount to serve four, add 2 T. of the juice, and all of the grated rind of one large green lime, and 1/2 t. powdered spearmint. Mix the whole gently; cover, and set in the refrigerator for an hour before using. Serve in sherbet glasses, garnished with Alpine strawberries.

BISCUIT TORTONI

2 c. milk
2 c. crumbs from almond macaroons
5 egg yolks
1/2 c. sugar

1 T. vanilla
1/2 c. sherry
1 pint heavy cream, whipped
grated green pistachio nuts
red candied cherries
candied angelica stems

Put milk and crumbs in the top of a double boiler, and cook over boiling water until very hot. Beat egg yolks with sugar until smooth and creamy. Add them to the hot mixture, stirring constantly until thickened. Cool, then chill. Add flavorings and whipped cream, and mix thoroughly. Pour mixture into 20 paper souffle cups (Dixie #51) and put them in the freezer. When they are partially frozen, remove from the freezer, a few at a time, and decorate the tops. First sprinkle grated green pistachio nuts over the top. Then make a flower, using candied angelica for stems and leaves, and for the flower, sliced candied cherries, bits of candied pineapple, and split blanched almonds. Return to freezer until frozen hard. Line a tin box which has a tight lid, with wax paper, and store biscuits in it. Return to freezer until ready to serve them.

BIBLIOGRAPHY

ARBER, AGNES, Herbals, Cambridge University Press, 1953

BAILEY, L. H., Manual of Cultivated Plants, MacMillan, N.Y., 1925

BAILEY, L. H., Hortus Second, MacMillan, N. Y., 1941

BARDSWELL, FRANCES A., The Herb Garden, A. C. Black, London, 1930

BRENDLE, T. R. Plant Names and Plant Lore Among the Pennsylvania Germans, Egypt, Pa., 1927

BROOK, RICHARD, A New Family Herbal, 1871

BUDGE, SIR ERNEST WALLIS, KT., The Divine Origin of the Craft of the Herbalist, Culpepper House, 7 Baker St., London, 1928

BUSH-BROWN, LOUISE, Men with Green Pens, Dorrance & Co., Phila., 1964

CHAUMETON, POIRET, CHAMBERET, Flore Médicale, Imprimerie de Panckoucke, Rue de Poitevins #14, Paris, 1833

CLARKSON, ROSETTA E., Green Enchantment, MacMillan, N.Y., 1940

CLARKSON, ROSETTA E., Magic Gardens, MacMillan, N.Y., 1941

CLARKSON, ROSETTA E., Herbs, MacMillan, N.Y., 1943

EARLE, ALICE MORSE, Old Time Gardens, MacMillan, N.Y., 1928

EVELYN, JOHN, Acetaria (reprint from first edition of 1699), Brooklyn Botanic Garden, Brooklyn, N.Y., 1937

FERNIE, W. T., Herbal Simples, Boericke & Tafel, Phila., 1897

FOLEY, DANIEL J., Herbs, Massachusetts State College, Amherst, Mass., 1914

FOX, HELEN M., Gardening with Herbs, MacMillan, N.Y., 1938

FUNK AND WAGNALLS, Dictionary of Folklore

GENLIS, STEPHANIE DE ST. AUBIN, La Botanique, Colburn, London and Paris, 1811

GERARD, JOHN, The Herball, London, 1597

GRAY, ASA, Manual of Botany (rewritten by Merritt Lyndon Fernald), 8th edition, 1950

GRIEVE, MAUD, A Modern Herbal, Vols. 1 and 2, Butler and Tanner, Ltd., Frome, England, 1931

HAMPTON, F. A., Flower and Leaf Scents, London, 1925

HOOKER AND JACKSON, Index Kewensis Vol. 1, Clarendon Press, Oxford, 1895

HYLL, Thomas (Didymus Mountaine), Gardener's Labyrinth, 1577

JEKYLL, GERTRUDE, Color Schemes in the Flower Garden, Butler and Tanner, Ltd., London

JOSSELYN, JOHN, New England Rarities, Boston, 1672

LEVERING, JOSEPH MORTIMER, History of Bethlehem, Times Publ. Co., Bethlehem, 1903

OHURI, JISABURO, Flora of Japan, Edited by Frederick Meyer, U.S. National Arboretum, 1965

POLUNIN, OLEG, Flowers of Europe, Oxford University Press, London, 1969

PARKINSON, JOHN, Paradisi in Sole, London, 1629 (First edition)

PARKINSON, JOHN, Paradisi in Sole, London, 1656 (Second edition)

QUINN, VERNON, Leaves, Frederick A. Stokes, 1937

QUINN, VERNON, Roots, Frederick A. Stokes, 1938

ROHDE, ELEANOUR SINCLAIR, Shakespeare's Wild Flowers, Medici Society, London, 1935

ROHDE, ELEANOUR SINCLAIR, Herbs and Herb Gardening, London, 1936

SINGLETON, ESTHER, The Shakespeare Garden, William F. Payson, N.Y., 1931

SOWERBY, JAMES, English Botany, Printed for the author by James Davis, 1740

STEMLER, DOROTHY C., Roses of Yesterday and Today, Watsonville, California, 1972

THOMAS, SIR W. BEECH, The Spectator, Vol. 5, Nov. 15, 1930

THOMSON, RICHARD, Old Roses for Modern Gardens, D. Van Nostrand, Inc., Princeton, N.J., 1959
WEBSTER, HELEN NOYES, Herbs, Adams Press, Lexington, Massachusetts, 1939
WILLIS, J. C., A Dictionary of Flowering Plants and Ferns, 7th edition, Cambridge University Press, 1966

GENERAL INDEX

Aconite, winter, 1
Agastache foeniculum, 82
Agastache rugosa, 82
Alecost, 8
Aloes, 3
Alpine strawberry, 1, 13, 14, 30, 34
Angelica, 44, 53, 81
Anise seed, 3
Armstrong, Dr. John, 36
Artemisia absinthium, 9

Bacon, Sir Francis, 37
Balm, lemon, 22, 44, 47
Basil, purple, 2
Basil, sweet, 2, 6, 14, 28, 73, 81
Basils, the, 38
Bay, sweet, 1, 37, 44, 49
Bedstraw, 78
Belladonna, 3
Benedictine monks, 5
Bergamot, 82
Bethlehem, Pa., 7
Bible leaf, 8
Black stem peppermint, 44, 46, 82
British Museum, 11
Bulleyn, William, 51
Burnet, 44, 46, 74
Buttercup, 4, 53

Caesar, Julius, 3, 55
Caraway thyme, 9
Cardamom, 3
Chamomile, 32, 82
Chervil, 14, 26
China, 3, 8
Chives, 1, 13, 16
Christmas Putz, 72
Christmas rose, 61

Clary sage, 9
Coltsfoot, 75
Community Putz, 67
Constantine the Great, 38
Continental Congress, 67
Coriander, 3, 44, 45
Corsican mint, 2, 75
Costmary, 7
Crete, 38
Crocus, saffron, 1, 61
Crown imperial, 59
Culpeper, Nicholas, 6, 37, 62
Cymbeline, 52

Dandelion, 4
Darbonne, Marc, 72
Dark opal basil, 28
De Materia Medica, 3
de Valois, Jeanne, 11
Dill, 6, 44, 45
Dioscorides, 3, 39
Dittany of Crete, 2, 76
Doctrine of Signatures, 4
Dwarf purple basil, 28

Eagle, Wisconsin, 8
Edward III, 11
Egypt, 3

Fairy, the (rose), 9
Fennel, sweet, 44, 47
Fines herbes, 7
Fletcher, John, 35
Franklin, Benjamin, 67

Gaige, Crosby, 72
Gardener's Labyrinth, 5
Garlic, 4, 74
Gemein Haus, 67

RECIPE INDEX